Rs 195/-

The Oxford India Illustrated

CHILDREN'S TAGORE

The Oxford India Collection is a series which brings together writings
of enduring value published by OUP.

Other titles include

The Illustrated Premchand: Selected Short Stories
The Oxford India Illustrated Corbett
The Second Oxford India Illustrated Corbett
The Oxford India Ghalib
The Oxford India Ramanujan
The Oxford India Premchand

The Oxford India Illustrated
CHILDREN'S TAGORE

Edited by
Sukanta Chaudhuri

OXFORD
UNIVERSITY PRESS

OXFORD
UNIVERSITY PRESS

YMCA Library Building, Jai Singh Road, New Delhi 110 001

Oxford University Press is a department of the University of Oxford. It furthers the
University's objective of excellence in research, scholarship, and education
by publishing worldwide in

Oxford   New York

Auckland   Cape Town   Dar es Salaam   Hong Kong   Karachi   Kuala Lumpur
Madrid   Melbourne   Mexico City   Nairobi   New Delhi   Shanghai   Taipei   Toronto

With offices in

Argentina Austria Brazil Chile Czech Republic France Greece Guatemala
Hungary Italy Japan Poland Portugal Singapore South Korea Switzerland
Thailand Turkey Ukraine Vietnam

Oxford is a registered trademark of Oxford University Press
in the UK and in certain other countries

Published in India by Oxford University Press, New Delhi

ISBN-13: 978-0-19-568417-9
ISBN-10: 0-19-568417-6

Illustrations by Rabindranath Tagore, Nandalal Bose, Asit Kumar Haldar
Paintings by Rabindranath Tagore, Rabindra Bhavan, Visva-Bharati

Typeset in Arrus BT 10.1/16 by Excellent Laser Typesetters, Delhi 110 034
Printed in India by Thomson Press (India) Ltd., New Delhi 110 020
Published by Oxford University Press
YMCA Library Building, Jai Singh Road, New Delhi 110 001

Publisher's Note

The poems, short stories and plays for children in this collection have been especially chosen from *Selected Writings for Children* (the Oxford Tagore Translations series) for their jest and appeal to young readers as well as Tagore fans. The illustrations, some by Tagore himself, others by members of the Shantiniketan community, draw on the ambience of his life and work. Again chosen especially for the volume from a variety of sources to complement each piece, they add verve and atmosphere to the writings.

The first section is a selection of verses, originally written in Bengali for children's textbooks, some delightfully nonsensical and fantastic ruminations of childhood. Childhood has always been a special place for Tagore whose interest in children's rhymes and tales from Bengal finds an echo in his poems.

The second is a collection of short stories containing motifs from fairy-tales reworked into real-life, adult experiences. Some of these have a moral, but are written in a playful manner that satirizes any serious message for the young reader. They are from a book called *Galpa-Salpa* (Chats), presented through conversations between a grandfather and a granddaughter.

The humourous plays or playlets contained in the next section act out certain Bengali words as in a game of charade. Some plays are hilarious, others poke fun at human foibles and social traits.

'My Childhood' was written purely for children, in the popular, spoken form of Bengali. These are accounts from Tagore's own childhood. As a writer, he was acutely aware of the social evils plaguing Bengal and India, and some of his poems and musings display this.

The last piece in the volume, 'Destruction', openly laments the loss of peace and love, when two nations are in conflict, set during the time of the second world war.

It is our hope that readers will enjoy this collection as well as other titles in the Oxford India Collection, which brings together writings of enduring value.

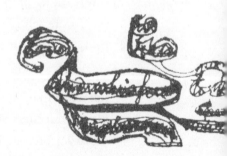

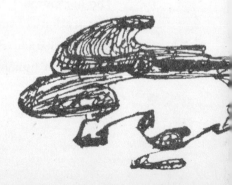

Contents

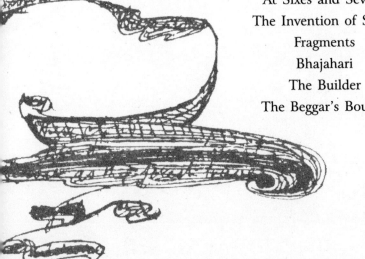

Grandfather's Holiday

Your holiday's among blue skies,
       your holiday's in the meadows,
Your holiday's along the steps
       down to the fathomless lake.
Under the tamarind tree it lies,
       in a corner of the barn,
Among the parul creepers,
       in every bush and brake.
Your holiday hope's a-tremble
       in the fields where young rice grows,
Your holiday joy is dancing
       in waves where the river flows.

I am your old grandfather:
       through spectacles I peer,
I'm caught up in the spider's web
       of all the world's affairs.
My holiday goes in the garb
       of your own holiday,
And in your voice, my holiday's
       sweet-piping music plays.
My holiday along the path
       of your dancing eyes is sped:

At the heart of your holiday,
      my holiday lies hid.

Your holiday's a ferry-boat
      where autumn plies the oars.
The shiuli grove your holiday-basket
      fills with its white flowers.
Your holiday companion
      is the dewy wind that breaks
Voyaging through the chilly night
      from Himalayan mountain-peaks.
And when among the opening buds
      the autumn dawning glides,
It comes draped in a mantle
      with your holiday colours dyed.

You leap, you run around my room:
      your holiday's in flood.
My piled-up work, my ledger-books
      all tremble at the thud.
O come and leap into my lap,
      come hug me in your play—
Set up a storm within my heart,
      my endless holiday.
He who grants you your holiday,
      who knows what He might mean?
My holiday I gain from you,
      and that is where I win.

—*Translated by Sukanta Chaudhuri*

Flowers

I couldn't see
Upon this tree
    A single flower
        Yesterday,
And now it's full:
Can the gardener tell
    How it could happen
        Just this way?

At hide and seek
The flowers peek,
    Within the trees
        They come and go.
Where do they hide,
Where do they bide
    With faces veiled?
        Does someone know?

Hidden from looks
Within their nooks
    They watch and wait
        With open ear,

Until the breeze
Among the trees
    Whistles a call
        They somehow hear.

At frantic pace
They scrub their faces
    For there's just
        No time to lose;
Then on they press
In coloured dresses
    From their homes,
        And out they cruise.

Where is that home
From which they come?
    Is it upon
        The earth close by?
Dada says no:
He seems to know
    It's far away,
        Up in the sky.

There all the day
Upon their way
    Colourful clouds
        Sail to and fro;
The sunlight pours
Through secret doors
    And in their midst
        The breezes blow.

—*Translated by Sukhendu Ray and Sukanta Chaudhuri*

The Voyage

Beside the landing-stage
A little boat would wait:
It danced among the ripples
When I went down to bathe.

But when I went today
The boat was far away,
Floating upon the ebb-tide
Among the waves at play.

So who can really tell
To what land it might sail—
Among what unknown people,
And how they dress and dwell.

Yet sitting here at home,
I wish that I could roam
Freely afloat just like the boat
And to new countries come,

Where by the distant seas
Among the ocean breeze,
Row upon row, there stand to view
Groves of coconut trees;

Or mountain peaks arise
Against the azure skies
Although no one can ever cross
The tracks of snow and ice;

Or unknown forests where
Among plants new and rare,
All sorts of strange new animals
Roam freely with no care.

Though many nights are gone,
The boat still wanders on:
Why must my father go to work
And not to lands unknown?

—Translated by Sukhendu Ray

The Runaway City

O what a dream of dreams I had one night!
I could hear Binu crying out in fright,
'Come quickly and you'll see a startling sight:
Our city's rushing in a headlong flight!'

Tottering and lurching
Calcutta goes marching
Beams and joists battling
Doors and windows rattling
Mansion houses dashing
Like brick-built rhinos crashing
Streets and roads jiggling
Like long pythons wriggling
While tumbling on their backs
Tramcars leave their tracks
Shops and marts go sprawling
Rising and then falling
One roof with another
Bang their heads together

Rolls on the Howrah Bridge[†]
Like a giant centipede
Chased by Harrison Road[†]
Breaking the traffic code
See the Monument[†] rock
Like a jumbo run amok
Waving its trunk on high
Against the troubled sky
Even our school in merry scoot
Books of maths in hot pursuit
The maps upon the walls aswing
Like a bird that flaps its wing
The school bell tolls on ding dong ding
Without a sense of when to ring

Thousands of people with Calcutta plead,
'Now stop your madness, where will all this lead?'
The city hurtles on and pays no heed,
Its walls and pillars dance with drunken speed.
But let it wander where it will, I say—
What if Calcutta travels to Bombay?
Agra, Lahore, or Delhi if it goes,
I'll sport a turban and wear nagra[†] shoes.
Or even England if right now it reaches,
I'll turn Englishman in hat, coat and breeches.
Then at some sound, my dream came to a pause
To find Calcutta where it always was.

—Translated by Sukhendu Ray

Bhotan-Mohan

Little Bhotan-Mohan dreams
    In a coach-and-four he courses.
His carriage is a banana-gourd,[†]
    And four bull-frogs his horses.

With a kingfisher to serve as guide,
To Chingrighata's bank he rides,
And there floats the banana-gourd
With a heap of bell-flowers laid aboard
    To sail upon the tides.
Bhotan-Mohan's full of glee:
    He laughs to split his sides.

—*Translated by Sukhendu Ray*

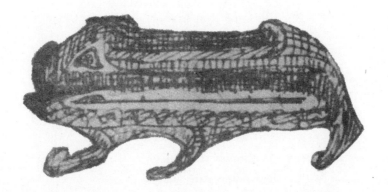

The Flying Machine

A mechanical bird!
How absurd!
A weird creature,
Fire-eater,
Sweeping the sky
Miles high,
Great wings sprawled—
What should you be called?

Did a monster kite
Or adjutant bird[†]
Lay a giant egg
That gave you birth?

Where is your nest?
In a banyan tree,
Or some iron branch
We never can see?

Why don't you sing
As you fly on your trips?

You whine and snivel
As though some devil
Beats you with whips.

Yet man has tamed
Your iron wings:
You're dumb, you're blind:
Caught in a bind
In your iron cage
Like a puppet on strings.

What a sad fate!
No savour, no sweet:
No voice of your own—
Hedged in by men
All day, all night.

You may gnash your teeth
And tower like a giant,
But we're not scared:
We stand defiant.

You carry people
On your back
Through night and day:
We little birds
Salute you—but
From far away.

—Translated by Sukhendu Ray

The Blaze

'Wake up, good sir!' the servant called.
The old man wouldn't heed at all.

He said, 'I can't go venturing:
My alarm clock has yet to ring.'

'Your house is on fire, can't you see?
Forget the alarm, get up and flee.'

'If I wake up too soon, I get
A dreadful pain inside my head.'

'Now your window's in a blaze:
Get going—there's no time to waste.'

'Don't pester me,' the old man groaned.
'Go away now, leave me alone.'

'Just as you wish,' his servant cried,
'But don't blame me if you get fried.'

'Your house is crumbling into dust.
Sleep on the street, if sleep you must.'

—Translated by Sukhendu Ray

The Tiger

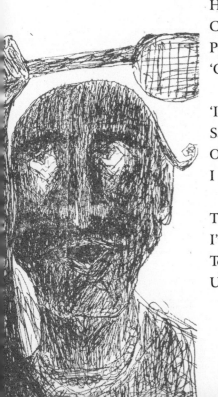

A black-striped tiger, big fat beast,
Marked down a man for his evening feast.
He saw his quarry take a broom,
And stalked him as he swept the room.
The man fled; but it came to pass
The tiger found a looking-glass
And saw his face, and raved and ranted:
'How were these stripes upon me planted?'

He left the room, and in a trice
Came where Putu was husking rice.
Puffing his whiskers out, he roared:
'Give me at once some glycerine soap!'

'I simply don't know what you mean,'
Said Putu. 'Where d'you think I've been?
Of lowly parents I have sprung:
I never learnt the English tongue.'

The tiger yelled, 'You're telling lies.
I've got the use of my two eyes.
To lose your stripes you couldn't hope
Unless you had some glycerine soap.'

Putu replied, 'You make me laugh.
I swear I've never touched the stuff.
I'm black and grimy, won't you grant?
Do I look like a memsahib's† aunt?'

The tiger said, 'You've got some gall:
I'll crunch you up, flesh, bones and all!'

'O no!' cried Putu in alarm,
'The very thought will do you harm.
For don't you know I'm lowly born,
To Mahatma Gandhi's following sworn?†
If on my flesh you come to feed,
You'll lose your caste with utmost speed!'

The tiger quaked in mortal funk.
'Don't come near me, or I'll be sunk!
In Tigerville my name will stink,
With no one could I eat or drink,
Or marry off a single daughter.
Why then, good-bye to soap and water!'

—*Translated by Sukhendu Ray*

The Palm Tree[†]

The palm tree stands
    On one leg, sees
    Past other trees
        Into the sky.
He wants to pierce
    The clouds so grey
    And soar away:
    But can he fly?

At length his wish
    He starts to spread
    Around his head
        In big round fronds:
He thinks they're wings,
    To let him roam
    Away from home,
        Breaking all bonds.

The livelong day
    The branches quiver,
Sigh and shiver—
        He thinks he flies,
In his own mind
    Skirting the stars,
    Racing afar
        Across the skies.

But when the wind
  Is still at last
  And the leaves hushed,
    Back homeward then
He turns his thoughts,
  And Mother Earth
  That gave him birth
    He loves again.

—Translated by Sukhendu Ray and Sukanta Chaudhuri

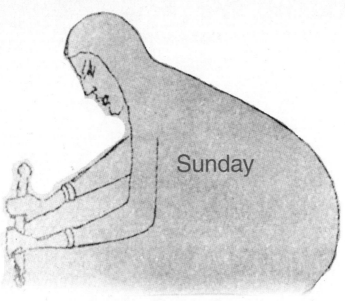

Sunday

Tell me mother:
The weekdays come so fast and thick—
Have they a car to reach so quick?
But why does Sunday take so long,
Behind the others trudging on?
Has she the farthest skies to cross?
Is her home as poor as yours?

Tell me mother:
The weekdays are an unkind lot:
To go back home they have no thought.
But why is Sunday so pursued
That she stays half the time she should?
Must she go back to do her chores?
Is her home as poor as yours?

Tell me mother:
The weekdays come with such long faces,
No child can stand such airs and graces.
But when at weekends I get up,
There's Sunday with her face lit up.
She starts to cry when back she goes:
Is her home as poor as yours?

—Translated by Sukhendu Ray

At Sixes and Sevens

শাপছাড়া

1

Old mother Khanto's grandma-in-law
Has the strangest sisters you ever saw.
Their saris on the stove they keep,
And saucepans on the clothes-horse heap.
From carping tongues to be at rest,
They hide inside an iron chest,
But at the window air their cash
    Without a jot of worry:
They put salt in their betel-leaves
    And quicklime† in their curry.

2

Four ruffians, all warts and blemishes,
Were raiding a shopkeeper's premises.
    They'd started to smash
    The till full of cash,
When who should arrive but the sergeant?
hey saw the police
    And whimpered, 'Oh please,
We're poor homeless waifs without guardian.
To better our prospects through knowledge,
    We made this intrusion
    Led by the delusion
That this was a free evening college.'

3

Don't worry, I'll do all the cooking today
　　While you take a rest from your toil.
Nidhu, just measure the water and rice,
　　And put the big pot on to boil.
　　　　I'll count out the platters:
　　　　But just to help matters,
The wife's very welcome to pick up a ladle
　　And stir at a dish while she's looking—
　　　　Or indeed, if she wants, have a go
　　　　At kneading and rolling the dough,
　　　　While Mahesh's part is
　　　　To bake the chapatis:[†]
But yes, I insist—as I've said from the start,
You must let me do all the cooking.

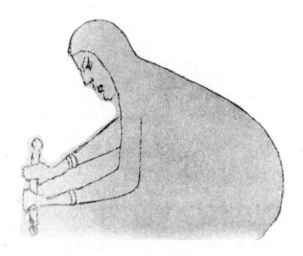

4

The King sits lost in silent meditation:
    While twenty sentries rend the air
    With cries of 'Quiet!' and 'Keep out there!'
The General bellows, as befits his station.

The Grand Vizier in his agitation
    Swishes his beard, and all the time
    Drums and bassoons and cymbals chime
Their warning notes in fearsome orchestration.

The solid earth shudders in consternation.
    The frightened beasts quiver and leap,
    And all the queens in order creep
Behind the curtains in their trepidation.

5

The famed research of Doctor Moyson
Filled the air with deadly poison.
    Until—O pity!—
    In all the city
He left just nine young men alive.
'What grand success!' he said. 'Just hear me
Tell you how it's done: but dear me,
    Who will attend
    Or comprehend
If no-one's able to survive?'

6

Asleep on the floor
With sonorous snore
    The Sultan enraptured all gazes;
      While wagging his beard
      The Minister steered
His voice through a raga's mazes.
Inspired by the bent of these musical courses,
The General commanding His Majesty's forces
Girded his waist in a colourful skirt
    And charmed the spectators with dances:
      The guards on parade
      Untunefully played
On flutes, having thrown down their lances.

7

Father Giraffe said, 'Really now, my boy,
To look at you gives little cause for joy.
My love grows less each time I view your body:
So tall up front, behind so squat and shoddy.'
'Look at yourself,' his son replied. 'It's true:
Nobody knows what Mother sees in you.'

8

If you set out for Khardah
And land up at Khulna instead,
    You may rage and strike terror,
    But that you're in error
Must clearly be taken as read.

If you want to weave garlands
But bring home a deal of sour berries,
    I'll hold with my powers
    That these are not flowers,
Although you drub me till I perish.

If you squat on a sofa
And tell me to give you a swing,
    You might land in a fury,
    But how can you query
I simply can't do such a thing?

If you feel a bit fey
As you sit in your dressing-room chair,
    And brush with great glee
    The crook of your knee,
    It's clearly my duty
    (Though it might sound snooty)
To point out it isn't your hair.

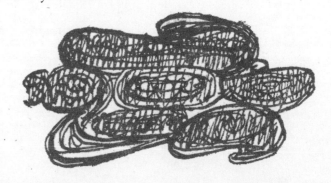

The Invention of Shoes

Said good king Hobu
To Minister Gobu,
    'I've pondered all night: is it just
That whenever my feet
Should land on the street
    They come to be sullied by dust?
Your wages you draw,
But you don't care a straw
    To serve the demands of the King:
It's a rank plot to foil me,
My own soil to soil me:
    I simply won't stand such a thing!
Unless you can find a solution,
You're all doomed to swift dissolution!'

The terrified Minister
At these words sinister
    Broke into cold sweat with fright:
The pandits† grew pale,
And the courtiers once hale
    Lay sleeplessly tossing all night.
In the Minister's home
There was weeping and gloom,
    The fires in the kitchen grew cold:

Till crazed with fears,
His beard drenched in tears,
  He fell at the King's feet, and told,
'But how can we live, if denied
The dust from your feet sanctified?'

'That's a question indeed,'
King Hobu agreed,
  'But "maybe" should come after "must".
We need to discourse
On this problem of yours,
  But meanwhile—get rid of the dust!
You're getting good money:
I don't think it funny
  You can't tackle problems like these.
There seems little point
Why I should appoint
  These scientists with long degrees.
So deal with the first things first,
Or else be prepared for the worst!'

Thus royally chided,
Poor Gobu decided
  To call the wise men of the land.
Each subtle mechanic
Was summoned in panic:
  They studied and brooded and scanned.
With spectacles perched
On the nose, they researched
  As they took nineteen barrels of snuff,
Then warned: if the crust
Of the earth lost its dust,
  You couldn't grow foodgrains enough.
'Why, what are you wise men worth?'
Said the King. 'Can't you tackle the dearth?'

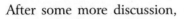

After some more discussion,
They found a solution—
 Which was, to buy millions of brooms.
The King couldn't breathe,
For the dust from the street
 Was driven right into his rooms.
The people that passed
Were blinded with dust,
 They coughed and they sneezed in a daze.
The dust floated down
And veiled all the town,
 The sun disappeared in the haze.
The King remarked, now really sore,
'To clear the dust, they've added more!'

So to dowse down the earth
And settle the dirt,
 Some two million watermen came:
They drained all the lakes
To fill water-bags,
 And boats couldn't sail on the stream.
The water-beasts died
As their element dried,
 While land-beasts struggled to swim:
All business was stuck
In the slime and the muck,
 And fever attacked every limb.
The King said, 'This army of asses
Has turned all the dust to morasses!'

So they held more talk,
And from every walk
    The wise men came to attend.
With reeling eyes
And dazed surmise
    They found of the dust no end.
One man had a thought
To lay out cloth,
    Or cover the land with mats:
Or day and night
To shut up tight
    The chamber where the King sat.
If they kept him enclosed all the time,
His feet couldn't land in the grime.

Said the King, 'That's neat!
It would guard my feet,
    But how could I govern my realm?
If I'm shut in a room,
The land meets its doom:
    I must have my hand on the helm.'
So they spoke again:
'Call the leathermen
    To sew up the earth in a sack.
'Twill make a great story
To his majesty's glory,
    And hold all the dust right back.
A simple device, if we can
Just find out a smart leatherman.'

For such leatherware
They looked everywhere,
    Abandoning all other chores:

But no craftsmen found,
Nor hides to go round,
    Even after they'd knocked on all doors.
But just at this while
There rose with a smile
    The leathermen's grizzled old chief.
'My lord, please permit
That I may submit
    A measure to bring you relief.
The whole earth you needn't ensheathe:
Just cover your own two feet.'

'Pooh! Were it so easy,
We wouldn't be busy,'
    The King said, 'pursuing our mission.'
'Let him be impaled,'
The Minister railed,
    'Or bind him and throw him in prison.'
But the old man sat down
At the foot of the throne,
    And in leather the royal feet dressed.
'Why,' Gobu now said,
'This was in my head:
    But how could the blighter have guessed?'
And that is how shoes were invented,
The earth saved, and Gobu contented.

Fragments

KNOWING LITTLE AND KNOWING MUCH

A thirsty ass went to a big lake's brink.
'This water's black!' he said, and wouldn't drink.
'Every ass sees I'm black,' the water cried.
'Only the wise man knows I'm really white.'

TRY FOR YOURSELF

'This honeycomb's so tiny,' said the wasp.
What makes the bee think it has cause to boast?'
'It's your turn now,' the bee replied. 'Do come:
Just try to make a smaller honeycomb.'

LITTLE HEARTS AND GREAT HEARTS

A tiny flower, of no worth at all,
Was growing from a cranny in the wall.
'Measly beggar!' cried every plant that grew.
But the rising sun called, 'Brother, how are you?'

AUDACITY

'How bold am I!' the rocket says. 'I race
To the stars, and fling my ashes in their face.'
'It doesn't stick to them,' the poet calls.
'It simply drops behind you as you fall.'

THE TEST OF EXPERIENCE

The thunderbolt says, 'When I call from far,
The people think it is the clouds that roar.
When I flash, "Lightning!" they cry down under.
But when I strike, they know I am the thunder.'

ON JUDGING OTHERS

The nose complains, 'The ear can't smell a thing:
It's good for nothing but to wear a ring.'
While the ear says, 'The nose can't hear a voice;
But when it sleeps, just listen to its noise!'

CAUSE FOR SUSPICION

Hear the fake diamond say, 'How big am I!'
That's why we think you might be just a lie.

WE ARE WHAT WE ARE

Turn and twist as you will, with all your might:
Your left hand's always to your left, your right hand to
your right.

Bhajahari

I had an uncle working in Hong Kong.
He brought for us a Chinese thrush that whistled a fine song,
    Sitting in its cage under a cover—
    A present for my mother.
Bhajahari would comb Nichinpur Wood
To bring it bags of grasshoppers for food,
And every cage-bird on the street would stir
Their feathers as he passed, to hear their whirr.
Some birds he fed on bugs, some rice, some swill;
Sprayed them with turmeric-water when they were ill.
'Watch me,' he'd say, 'I fill the bugs with fright:
The dragonflies can't sleep a wink all night,
And at my sound, the beetles and the crickets
Hide in the leaves when I stomp through the thickets.'

One spring he came to Mother for to say,
'Tomorrow is my daughter's wedding day.'
    How funny seemed his words!
    That Bhaja of the birds
Should have a daughter, or that she should wed
With a red silken veil over her head!
'Will it be very grand?' I asked. He cried,
'Of course! Among my friends I have my pride.

Some sit on perches, some in cages barred—
I'll send them each an invitation card.
They'll feast on chick-peas, millet-flour with curds,
Juicy fat grasshoppers—why, all the birds
    Such an uproar will make,
    The neighbours all the night will lie awake.
I'll feed the mynahs chillies till they bawl:
The cockatoo will boom its loudest call,
The pigeons pout their throats out as they coo,
The crabby starlings add a squawk or two.
The parakeets and koels will be there,
Their screeches shutting out the marriage prayer.
    When the groom's father hears
The parrots scream, he'll turn and stop his ears!'

The Builder

I'm not so small as I might look:
    I'm thirty summers old.
I'm not your Shirish,† Mother dear—
    Noto is what I'm called.

On Tamiz Mian's bullock cart
    Each day to town I ride.
From then until the shadows gather,
I lay one brick upon another
    And build a wall, exactly as I like.

You think I'm only at my play,
Making houses out of clay—
    It's just not so, they're really proper homes.
And don't think either that they're small:
They rise to be three storeys tall,
    With columns and with domes.

But if you think of asking me
Why I should stop at only three,
    I really can't reply:
Why not sixty, seventy floors,
Brick on brick, until it rose
    Right up into the sky?

Higher and higher, yet more far
Until the rafters touch the stars
    And you can't see the top?
I puzzle over this myself:
    Why need I ever stop?

I clamber up onto the roof
    Along the scaffold-frame:
I really think it's better fun
    Than any sort of game.
The roofbeaters† sing at their work,
    While on the street down there
The cars rush by, the pedlar-man
Clangs upon his pots and pans,
    The fruitseller goes crying out his ware.

At half-past four, you hear a shout:
Boys come rushing, school is out—
    They raise the dust as down the road they run.

The light begins to fail at last,
The crows go flapping to their nest
        At the setting of the sun.

So when the day is at an end,
Down from the scaffold I descend,
        Back to my village come:
You see that post left of the pond?
        That's where I have my home.

But if you think of asking me
Why a straw hut my home should be
        When I build mansions high—
Why should my house not rise as tall,
Or be the biggest one of all?
        I really can't reply.

The Beggar's Bounty

When famine stalked Shravasti† town,
Filling the air with tears and groans,
The Buddha to his disciples came   and spoke in turn to each by name:
'Who will take on the load
To give the hungry food?'

The rich merchant Ratnakar Seth
Heard the plea, and hung his head.
'My lord,' he cried, joining his hands,   'to feed the vast and hungry bands
Of this great town of ours,
Is not within my powers.'

Next the warrior Jaysen spake:
'Your task I happily would take
Upon my head, and make it good   were it the shedding of my blood
Or my heart's flesh to carve:
In my own home, we starve.'

Dharmapal, next to relate,
Cried, 'Alas my hapless fate!
The spectre of the drought has killed   the golden harvest of my field—
I am nothing today.
My taxes I scarce can pay.'

Each at the others' faces stares:
Not one to make an answer dares.
Out of that silent meeting-place,   only the Buddha's pitying gaze,

Like the evening star, looked down
Upon the suffering town.

Slowly at last then, blushing red,
With anguished tears and lowered head,
Anathapindada's† daughter rose.   She touched the Buddha's feet, and spoke
In humble tones yet free
To all the company:

'I, Supriya, lowliest mendicant,
Take upon me your commandment.
All those who cry and lack for food,   they are the children of my brood:
I take upon my head
The task to keep them fed.'

Amazement broke out in the ranks:
'Begging daughter of a begging monk,
Tell us what foolish pride of self   has made you take upon yourself
A task so vast and grave.
What riches do you have?'

She answered, bowing low to all:
'Nothing except my begging-bowl.
Resourceless woman that I am,   that very fact will make me claim
Largesse from all of you,
The master's will to do.

'I can command at every door
The treasure of my endless store.
You can perpetuate, if you wish,   the bounty of my begging-dish:
The world shall live through your alms,
And the famine's pang find calm.'

The King's Palace

'Aunt Iru was a very clever girl: wasn't she, Grandpa?' asked Kusmi.

'Of course she was—cleverer than you are!'

Kusmi stopped short. She sighed a little and said, 'So that's why she managed to cast a spell on you.'

'You've got it all wrong. What gave you the idea that you must be clever in order to charm people?'

'What then?'

'You need to be silly, that's what. There's a simpleton deep inside everyone: that's where you must appeal to charm them, by being truly silly. That's why love is called the art of charming.'

'Tell me how it's done.'

'I've no idea. I was only going to tell you what happens when someone is put under that kind of spell.'

'All right, carry on.'

'I've always had a great weakness, you see: I'm amazed by every little thing. That's what Iru took advantage of. She kept amazing me all the time.'

'But wasn't Aunt Iru younger than you are?'

'Of course she was, by a full year at least. But she was wise beyond her years—I could never catch up with her. She ruled over me as though I hadn't yet cut my teeth. And I could only stare open-mouthed at everything she did.'

'What fun!'

What fun indeed. She worked me up into a
state with a story about a king's seven-mansioned
palace. I never found out where it was—she alone
knew the secret. I was going through the Third
Reader then, I remember. I asked my teacher about it,
but he only laughed and tweaked my ears.
I would often plead with Iru: 'Tell me where the palace is.'
She would only open her eyes very wide and say, 'Right here in this
house.'
I would gape and say, 'No, really—in this house? Show me where it is!'
But she always said, 'You can't see it unless you know the magic
words.'
'Then teach me the magic words, please,' I would beg her. 'I'll give
you that seashell I splice mangoes with.'
'It's forbidden to tell them to anyone,' she would reply.
'Why, what'll happen if you tell me?' I would ask.
But she would only gasp, 'Oh, goodness me!'
I never found out what would happen if she told me, but her attitude
made me shudder. I decided to shadow her one day when she next
went to visit the palace; but she seemed to go only while I was at
school. I asked her once why she couldn't go at any other time, but
she only said, 'Oh, goodness me!', and I was too scared to press her
any more.

She would give herself great airs when she managed to impress me.
Sometimes, when I had just returned from school, she would blurt out:
'You won't believe what happened today.'
'What was it?' I would ask, all excited.
And she would reply, 'Shan't tell you.'
I suppose it was best that way. I never got to know what happened, so
I could go on dreaming of fantastic things.
She would go off to the Hurry-Scurry Fields while I was asleep. A
winged horse grazed in the meadows there, and whisked away anyone
who came there up into the clouds.

I would clap my hands with joy when I heard this, and say, 'What fun that must be!'

And she would reply, 'Fun indeed! Oh, goodness me!'

Her expression scared me so much that I never got round to asking what the danger might be.

She had even seen fairies keeping house, and not very far from our home either. She had seen them in the gloom among the thick roots of the old banyan tree on the east bank of our pond. They lived only on nectar, and she had made friends by gathering flowers for them. But she only went to visit their houses when we boys were doing our lessons with Nilkamal-Master[†] on the south balcony.

'What would happen if you went at some other time?' I would ask her.

'The fairies would turn into butterflies and fly away,' she would tell me.

She had many other things in her magic bag, but it was that unseen palace that really fascinated me. Just think—a mysterious palace tucked away in our very own house, perhaps right next to my own bedroom, only I could never catch a glimpse of it as I didn't know the magic words! I often went with Iru to the mango grove, plucked green mangoes for her, even bribed her with my precious seashell. She would peel the mangoes and eat them with dill leaves; but every time I asked her about the magic words, pat came the reply: 'Oh, goodness me!'

Then Iru got married and went off to her in-laws, and the secret went with her. And I grew too old to go looking for palaces, so I never found the place after all. Since then I have seen lots of real palaces from afar, but a palace tucked away near my own house—oh, goodness me!

The Big News

'You promised to tell me all the big news of the
world, Grandpa,' Kusmi reminded me. 'How else can I
be educated?'
'The bag of big news is too heavy to carry around,' said
Grandfather. 'It's stuffed so full of rubbish.'
'Well, leave out the rubbish and tell me the rest, can't you?'
'That would leave very little substance: you'd think it wasn't big news
at all. But it would be the real news.'
'That's all right, give me the real news then.'
'So I will. You're a lucky girl. If you were reading for your BA degree,
your table would be piled high with rubbish; you'd have to trundle
round a load of notebooks crammed with lies and nonsense.'
'All right, Grandpa. Tell me some really big news, and try to keep it
very short,' said Kusmi. 'Let's see how good you are at it.'
'All right, listen on.'

It was peaceful on board the merchant boat. Then a violent quarrel
broke out between the oars and the sail. The oars rattled up in a body
and laid their case before the boatman. 'We shan't put up with this
any more,' they said. 'That sail of yours, all puffed up with pride, calls
us a vulgar mob—and all because we're lashed to the planks down in
the hold and forced to wade through the water night and day, while
he merrily goes his own way, with no hand to
push him along. He thinks that makes him a

superior person. You must decide once and for all who's worth more
to you. If we're really of no consequence, we'll resign all together. Let's
see how you manage your boat without us!'

The boatman sensed trouble. He took the oars aside and whispered to
them, 'Don't pay him the slightest attention, my brothers! He's just a
windbag. Why, if you strong men didn't do your utmost, this boat
wouldn't move at all! That sail's a toff, an empty upper-deck showoff.
One strong gust of wind and he crumples up in a heap, without so
much as a flutter—whereas I know you'll stay by my side through thick
and thin. It's you who carry that monstrous load of vanity through all
weathers. How dare he call you such vile names!'

But now the boatman was afraid the sail might have heard his words.
So he went up to him and whispered in his ears, 'Dear Mr Sail, there's
no one to compare with you. Who says you only run a boat? That's
just crude labour, quite unworthy of you. You simply follow your
noble fancy, while your lackeys bring up the rear. Maybe you sag a
little now and then when you're out of breath, but what of that?
Brother, don't listen to the vulgar prattle of those oars. I've fixed them
so tightly that labour they must, no matter how much they grumble
and splash about!'

At this the sail puffed up his chest and yawned as he looked up at
the clouds.

But the signs don't augur well for him. Those oars are tough-boned.
They've been lying on their sides a long time, but they'll stand up
straight and hit back hard one of these days. The sail's pride will be

shattered. The world will learn that it's the oars that move the boats through tide and storm and rain.

'Is that all?' asked Kusmi. 'Was that your big news? You must be joking.'
'It sounds like a joke now,' said Grandfather, 'but one day it'll be seen for the big news that it is.'
'What's going to happen then?'
'Why, your Grandpa will fall in with those oars and learn to keep time with them!'
'And what about me?'
'You'll go about oiling the oars where they creak too much.'
'You understand now, don't you?' asked Grandfather. 'The really important news is always tiny, like a seed. It takes time for a big tree to grow out of it, branches and all.'
'Oh yes, I understand,' said Kusmi.
It was evident from her face that she hadn't understood at all. But Kusmi has the virtue of never admitting that to her Grandpa. It's best not to tell her she's not as clever as her Aunt Iru used to be.

The Fairy

'You keep spinning such tall tales, Grandpa,' said Kusmi. 'Why don't you tell me a true story for a change?'

I said, 'There are two classes of things in this world. One is the true, the other is the more-than-true. I deal with the more-than-true.'

'Grandpa, people say they can't understand you at all.'

'They're quite right,' I agreed. 'But the fault is theirs, not mine.'

'Why don't you explain what you mean by the more-than-true?'

'Why, just look at yourself,' I told her. 'Everybody knows of you as Kusmi. And that's perfectly true—there are proofs enough. But I have come to know that you're a fairy from fairyland. That's more-than-true.'

Kusmi was pleased. 'But how did you find out?' she asked.

I said: 'Once you had an exam the next day, and you were sitting up in bed, learning your geography, until at last you began to nod. Your head sank upon the pillow, and you fell fast asleep. It was a full-moon night, and the moonlight came pouring in through the window and fell on your face and your sky-blue sari. I saw quite plainly that the Fairy King had sent a scout to look for his runaway fairy. He came sailing past my window, and his white shawl swept into the room. He looked you down from head to toe, but couldn't decide whether you were that runaway fairy. He thought you might be a fairy of this very earth: you might be too heavy for them to carry away. Meanwhile the moon climbed higher; the room was cast in shadow. Standing under the shishu tree, the scout shook his head and went back. Then I knew you were a fairy from fairyland, trapped down here by the weight of the earth.'

'How did I reach here from fairyland, Grandpa?' Kusmi asked.

I said, 'You were skyriding on a butterfly's back in a forest of asphodel, when you caught sight of a ferry-boat moored at the horizon. It was made of white clouds, and it rocked in the wind. You got into the boat on a fancy, and it drifted off till it reached the earth, where your mother picked you up in her arms.'

Kusmi clapped her hands in delight. 'Is all this really true, Grandpa?'

'There you go again!' said I. 'Who ever said it was true? What do I care for the truth? This is more-than-true.'

Then she asked, 'Can't I ever go back to fairyland?'

'Perhaps you can,' I answered, 'if a strong breeze from those parts should touch the sails of your dream boat.'

'Suppose that does happen, how shall I find my way back? Is fairyland very far away?'

'It's very close by,' I replied.

'How close?'

'As close as you are now to me. You won't even have to get out of this bed to go there. Just wait for another night when the moonlight comes through the window, and if you look out, you shan't have any doubts left at all. You'll see the cloud-ferry floating down the moonbeams towards you. But that boat won't do for you any more: you're an earth-bound fairy now. You'll leave your body behind in bed, and only your spirit will go with you. Your truth will remain here on earth, while your more-than-true soars up, up and away, where none of us can reach.'

'Very well then,' said Kusmi, 'on the next full-moon night I'll watch the sky from the window. Grandpa, will you hold on to my hand and come with me?'

'No, but I can tell you the way even as I sit right here. I have the power—I'm a dealer in things more-than-true.'

More-than-true

'Grandpa, that more-than-truth you were talking about the other day—
is it to be found only in fairyland?'

'Not at all, my dear,' said I. 'There's a lot of it in this world of ours.
You only need to look. But of course you must have the eye to
spot it.'

'Can you see it?'

'That's one power I do have. I suddenly catch sight of things that
aren't meant to be seen. When you sit by my side learning your
geography, I remember my own studies. That Yang-tse-kiang river of
yours—every time I read the name, it conjured up a kind of geography
that was absolutely no use in passing exams. Even now I can see that
long caravan with its enormous loads of silk. I once found a place on
the back of one of those camels.'

'Come off it, Grandpa! I know you never rode a camel in your life!'

'Really, Didi, you ask too many questions.'

'Never mind, go on. What happened then? Where did you get a
camel from?'

'There, another question already!—I never worry about finding camels:
I simply climb on to one. Whether or not I visit other lands, nothing
stops me from travelling. That's the way I am.'

'Well, what happened after that?'

'After that I passed through so many grand cities one by one—
Fuchung, Hangchow, Chungkung; I crossed so many deserts, finding my
way at night by the stars. And then I came upon the jungle at the foot
of the Ush-khush Mountains†—past olive groves, through vineyards,
along pine forests. I fell among thieves, and a great white bear rose on
its hind legs in front of me.'

'When did you find the time to wander like that?'

'Oh, I travelled while the class was busy with their exams.'

'But how did you pass the exams then?'

'That's easy—I never did pass.'

'All right, get on with the story.'

'Now shortly before I set out on that journey I had read in the *Arabian
Nights* about the beautiful princess of China. And wonder of wonders! I
chanced upon her in my travels. It was on the bank of the Fuchao
river. The landing-place was paved in marble, leading up to a pavilion
of blue stone. There was a champak tree on each side, with a stone
lion at its foot. Incense burned in gold censers, and the smoke rose in
coils. One maid was doing up the princess' hair, while two others
fanned her, one with a yak's tail. I somehow appeared before her all of
a sudden. She was feeding her milk-white peacock with pomegranate
seeds. She gave a start and asked: 'Who are you?'

'I remembered in a flash: I was the crown prince of Bengal!'

'How could that be? You were only—'

'Questions again! I'm telling you I was the crown prince of Bengal
for that day, and that's what saved me: otherwise she would have
had me thrown out there and then. Instead, she gave me tea in a
golden cup—tea laced with chrysanthemums, bearing the most
marvellous scent.'

'Did she marry you after all that?'

'Now that's something very secret. Nobody knows to this day.'

Kusmi clapped her hands: 'It happened, I know it happened! You
married the princess in the very grandest way.'

Plainly she would be very upset if it didn't work out like that. 'Yes, in the end she married me all right. I got my Princess Angchani, and half the kingdom of Hangchow as well. And then—'

'Then what? Did you set off on your camel again?'

'Else how did I come back to be your Grandpa? Yes, I climbed back on to my camel, the camel that went nowhere. The fusung bird flew carolling over my head.'

'The fusung bird! Where does it live?'

'Oh, it lives nowhere, but its tail feathers are blue, its wings yellow, and there's a brown patch on its shoulders. They flew off in great numbers, and perched on the hachang tree.'

'I've never heard of the hachang tree.'

'Nor have I—I only just thought of it as I was telling you the story. That's the sort of person I am: I'm never ready beforehand—I tell you whatever I see, even as I'm seeing it. Today my fusung bird has flown across the sea. I haven't had news of it for ages.'

'But what about your marriage? And the princess?'

'I won't answer you there, my dear, so you'd better stop asking. And anyway, you mustn't let it upset you. You weren't even born then, remember.'

The Rats' Feast

'It's an outrage,' said the boys. 'We shan't
study under a new teacher!'
They were going to have a new Sanskrit
teacher, Kalikumar Tarkalankar[†] by name.
The vacation was over, and the boys were on
the train going back to school. A wag had
already changed the new teacher's name into
Kalo Kumro Tatka Lanka, 'Black pumpkin and
red-hot chilli', and made up a rhyme called
'The Sacrifice of the Black Pumpkin.'[†] They
were belting it out in chorus.
At Arkhola an elderly gentleman boarded the train.
He had a bedroll with him, a few bundles, a big trunk
and two or three large earthen pots, their tops bound
with cloth. A tough boy, whom everyone called Bichkun, yelled at
him at once: 'Get down, you old fool, there's no room here. Go to
another carriage.'
The old man said, 'The whole train's packed, there isn't a seat to be
found anywhere. Don't worry, I'll sit in a corner here; I won't trouble
you at all.'
He left the whole seat to them, rolled out his bedding on the floor, and
settled down on it. Then he turned to them and asked, 'Where are you
going, my sons, and for what?'
'To settle somebody's hash for him,' said Bichkun.

'And who might he be?' asked the old man.

'*Kalo Kumro Tatka Lanka*,' came the reply, and the boys merrily took up the chant:

> Black pumpkin and red hot chilli,
> We'll soon make him look pretty silly!

At Asansol the train stopped for a while, and the old man got down to have a wash. The moment he came back Bichkun shouted, 'Get off this coach if you know what's good for you, mister.'

'Why, what's the matter?'

'There are rats all over the place.'

'Rats! You don't say so!'

'Look for yourself. See what they've done to your pots over there!'

The old gentleman saw that all the sugar balls in one pot were gone, and not a morsel was left of the sweets[†] in another.

'They've run off with whatever you had in that bundle of yours too,' said Bichkun.

The bundle had held five ripe mangoes from his garden.

'Poor creatures,' he said with a smile, 'they must have been very hungry!'

'Oh no, they're always like that,' Bichkun told him. 'Even if they're not hungry, they'll tuck in all the same!'

The boys roared with laughter: 'That's right, mister. If there had been anything more they'd have eaten that too!'

'It's my fault,' said the man. 'If I'd known there would be all these rats on the train, I'd have come better stocked.'

The boys felt rather disappointed when they saw the old man wasn't angry. They would have enjoyed seeing him lose his temper.

At Bardhaman there was an hour's wait. They had to change trains. The gentleman said, 'I won't trouble you young men any more. I can find a seat in another coach this time.'

'Oh no, you must come with us,' they clamoured. 'If there's anything left in your bundles, we'll guard it all the way. We promise you won't lose anything else!'

'Very well,' said the gentleman. 'You go ahead and board the train;
I'll be along in a minute.'

They climbed into the new train. A little later a sweet-seller came
trundling his cart to their window, the gentleman beside him.

He handed each of them a paper bag full of sweets, saying, 'This time
the rats won't go hungry.' The boys gave a hurrah. Next a mango-
seller came along with his basket, and mangoes were added to the
feast.

The boys asked the gentleman, 'Tell us where you're going and why.'

'I'm looking for a job,' he told them. 'I'll go wherever I can find one.'

'What sort of work can you do?' they asked.

'I'm a schoolteacher,' he said. 'I teach Sanskrit.'

They clapped their hands. 'Then you must come to teach in our
school!'

'But why should they have me?'

'We'll make them,' they assured him. 'We shan't let *Kalo Kumro Tatka
Lanka* set foot in the neighbourhood, you'll see.'

'You're making things difficult for me.
Suppose your secretary doesn't like me?'

'He'd better—else we'll all quit the
school together!'

'Very well then, my sons—take me
to your school.'

The train puffed into the station.
The secretary of the school
committee was waiting in person
on the platform. Seeing the old
gentleman get off, he came up to
meet him.

'Welcome, Master Tarkalankar, sir.
Your rooms are ready for you.'
And he bent down to touch the
old man's feet.

That Man

Down the ages, God has gone on creating human beings in their
millions and billions. But no, that wasn't good enough for those
humans. They said, 'We want to produce our own human beings.'
So alongside God's games with his living dolls, humans began their
own games with dolls they had made themselves. And then children
began to say, 'Tell us a story'—in other words, make human beings out
of words. Thus were devised the countless king's sons and minister's
sons, favourite queens and neglected queens, fables of mermaids, tales
of the Arabian Nights, the adventures of Robinson Crusoe. These
creations kept multiplying in pace with the world's population. Even
grown-ups began to say, when they had a day off from work, 'Make
us some human beings.' And so the epic Mahabharata[†] was prepared
in eighteen books. Now a host of story-makers are kept busy in
every land.

At my granddaughter's command, I've been involved for some time
in this game of people-making. They are play-people, so it doesn't
matter whether they are true or false. My listener is nine years old,
and the story-teller has crossed seventy. I started my work all on my
own, but Pupu joined in when she found the stuff I worked with was
very light. I did call in another man to help me, but more of him later.
Many tales start with 'Once there was a King.' But I'm beginning my
tale with 'There is a Man.' My stories are nothing like what people
mean by stories. This Man never rode on horseback across the vast
fairy-tale fields of Tepantar.[†] Instead, he came to my room one evening

after ten o'clock at night, when I was reading a book. He said, 'Dada, I'm very hungry.'

Now in all these tales about princes, we never hear of a hungry prince. Nonetheless, I was rather pleased that my character should be hungry at the start of my story—because, you see, it's easy to make friends with a hungry person. To please him, you don't have to travel farther than the end of the lane to buy him some food.

I discovered that my Man was fond of good food. He'd ask for curried fish heads, shrimps with gourd, or a savoury dish of fish-bones and vegetables. If you gave him malai† from Barabazar,† he'd lick the bowl clean. As for ice-cream, it was a treat to see him relish one: he would remind me of the Majumdars' son-in-law.

It was raining rather hard one day. I was painting in my room: a landscape of the wide open fields you see in these parts,† with a red-clay road going due north; an uneven piece of fallow land to the south with curly-headed wild date-palms; a few toddy-palm trees in the distance, staring avidly at the sky like beggars; behind them a dense black cloud, like a huge blue tiger ready to pounce on the sun in mid-sky. All this was I painting, mixing colours in a bowl, swishing my paintbrush.

There was a shove at the door. When I opened it, in came—not a bandit, not a giant, not even a general's son—but that Man. He was dripping water, his dirty shirt stuck to his body, the end of his dhoti was splashed with mud, and his shoes were just like two lumps of clay.

'How now!' I said.

'It was dry and sunny when I left home,' he said. 'I got caught in the rain midway. Can I have that bedspread of yours? I could then get out of these wet clothes and wrap myself in it.'

Before I could say anything, he snatched my Lucknow bedspread, dried his head with it and wrapped it around himself. It was lucky I didn't have my precious Kashmir jamewar† on the bed.

Then he said, 'Dada, let me give you a song.'

What could I do? I abandoned my painting. He began to sing the old-fashioned song:

> *Just think, Shrikanta, you handsome young lover,*
> *Grim death will approach and your life will be over.*†

From my expression, he suspected that it wasn't going well. 'How do you like it?' he asked.

'Look,' I told him. 'As long as you live, you'd better remove yourself far, far away from human habitation if you want to practise the scales. After that it's up to Chitragupta,† who writes down all your deeds in a fat register to charge you with after you're dead. That's if he's able to stand your song.'

He piped up, 'Pupe Didi takes music lessons from a Hindustani ustad.† How about my joining her?'

'If you can persuade Pupe Didi to agree, there shouldn't be any problem,' I replied.

'I'm scared stiff of Pupe Didi,' he said.

At this point Pupe Didi, who was listening, broke into peals of laughter. She was delighted by the idea that anyone could be scared stiff of her. She found it very pleasing, as do all the strong men of the world.

But being tender-hearted, she said, 'Tell him he needn't be afraid. I won't say anything to him.'

'Is there anyone who's not afraid of you?' I asked her. 'Don't you drink a bowlful of milk twice a day? Look how strong it's made you. Don't you remember how that tiger met you brandishing a stick, and ran away with its tail tucked under him to hide under Aunt Nutu's bed?' Our heroine was ecstatic. She reminded me of that other time when a bear, trying to escape from her, fell into the bathtub.

The history of my Man, that I was so far putting together all by myself, now took on additions from Pupe's hands. If I were to tell her that the Man came to see me at three in the afternoon to ask for a razor and an empty biscuit tin, she would add that he had also borrowed her crochet hook.

All stories have a beginning and an end, but my story of 'There is a Man' has no end: it just runs on. His sister falls ill and he goes to fetch a doctor. A cat scratches the nose of his dog Tommy. He jumps onto the back of a bullock-cart and gets into a row with the carter. He takes a tumble in the backyard near the pump and breaks an old brahman lady's earthen pitcher. During a football match when Mohan Bagan[†] is playing, his pocket gets picked clean of three and a half annas, so he can't buy sweets from Bhim Nag's[†] shop on the way home. Instead he goes to see his friend Kinu Choudhuri, and asks for fried shrimps and curried potatoes.

And so it goes on, day after day. Pupe adds how one afternoon, he walks into her room and asks to borrow a cook-book from her mother's cupboard because his friend Sudhakanta Babu wants to cook banana flowers. Another day he begs for Pupe's perfumed coconut hair-oil as he's afraid he's going bald. Yet another day he goes over to Din-Da's[†] hoping to hear him sing, but finds him asleep, snuggling his bolster.

Of course this Man of ours has a name; but it's known to just the two of us and can't be disclosed to anybody else. That's where the real fun of our story lies. The king who lived once upon a time had no name; neither did the prince. And that lovely princess, whose hair reached down to the floor, whose smile showered gems and her tears pearls—no one knows her name either. They were quite nameless, yet they are well-known in every home. This person of ours we just call *Se*—'He', or 'That Man'. When a stranger asks his name, we two just smile and look knowingly at each other. Sometimes Pupe says teasingly, 'Have a guess. It starts with a P.' And people guess it to be Priyanath, or Panchanan, or Panchkari, or Pitambar, or Paresh, or Peters, or Prescott, or Pir Bux, or Pyar Khan.

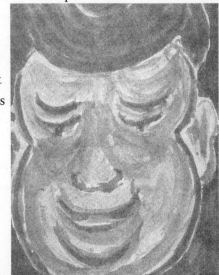

As I put down my pen at this point, someone piped up at once,
'I hope that's not the end of the story.'

Story! What story? Our hero isn't a prince; he's just an ordinary Man.
He eats and sleeps, has a job in an office, likes to see movies. His
story is simply his daily routine, which is like everybody else's. If you
can build him up clearly in your minds, you'll see him wolfing down
rasgullas† in the front porch of a sweetshop, with syrup dripping from
the bottom of the packet onto his grubby dhoti. That's his story. If
you ask, 'What happened then?', I'd say he jumped onto a tramcar,
found he had no money, and so jumped off again. And then? Much,
much more of the same sort happens then. He goes from Barabazar to
Bowbazar, from Bowbazar on to Nimtala.†

Someone among the listeners said, 'This Man seems to be an unstable
character: he can't find shelter in Barabazar, or Bowbazar, or Nimtala.
Can't you make up a story about his waywardness?'

'Well,' I said, 'if one can, one can; if one can't, one can't.'

'Let's have your story then,' the listener said. 'Just whatever comes to
your mind—with neither head nor tail, sum nor substance.'

Now that really would be bold. God's creation is strictly ruled by order
and system: everything there must be as it should be. It becomes quite
intolerable. Let's make fun of Grandfather God, who created this dull
system, and do it in such a way that he can't punish us. My story lies
quite outside his domain.

Our Man was sitting quietly in a corner. He whispered in my ear, 'Dada,
have a go, write whatever you want about me: I shan't take you to court.'
I now need to say something about this Man.

The main prop of the serial story that I keep telling Pupu Didi is a
Man built wholly out of words, a Man named after a pronoun—'He'.
That's why I can make up any stories I like around him and no
questions asked. But as evidence to back up my chaotic creations, I've
had to find a man of flesh and blood. If I'm threatened with a literary
lawsuit, this man is ready to stand up and testify in my favour. He
doesn't mind what he says. Given a hint, even by a petty lawyer like
me, he'll swear without batting an eyelid that a crocodile once caught

his topknot between its jaws when he was taking a dip in the holy Ganga during the Kumbha Mela[†]—the one held in Kanchrapara.[†] The topknot went down with the crocodile, but the rest of the man, like a flower cut off its stalk, managed to reach dry land. If you wink at him a little more, he can shamelessly declare that some English divers from a man-o'-war rummaged in the mud for seven months and finally brought up his topknot, all but a few hairs. He tipped them three and a quarter rupees. If Pupu Didi still asks 'What happened next?', he'll immediately continue that he went to see the great Doctor Nilratan Sarkar[†] and implored him, 'Please, Doctor Babu, give me some medicine to fix my topknot, otherwise I can't tie a flower to it.' The doctor applied a powerful ointment that a Holy Man had given him. Now his topknot keeps growing recklessly, like an endless earthworm. When he wears a turban, it swells like a blown-up balloon; when he rests his head on a pillow, his topknot forms a canopy like a giant mushroom. He has to pay a barber full time to shave his head every three hours.

If the hearer is still curious for more, he'll continue his story with a sad face. He'll say he found the Surgeon-General of the Medical College waiting with his shirtsleeves rolled up, bent on drilling a hole at the root of his topknot, plugging it with a rubber stopper and then sealing it with wax to prevent the topknot from ever growing again in this world or the next. He was afraid that this drastic treatment might carry him straight to the next world, so he refused to oblige.

This Man of ours is a rare bird, one in a million: an unparalleled genius in making up lies. I'm very lucky to have found such an artful disciple for my outlandish yarn-spinning. Sometimes I present to Pupe Didi this strange creature from my tale. At the sight of him, Pupe Didi's large eyes grow even larger. She's so pleased that she orders hot jalebis[†] for him from the market. The Man is inordinately fond of jalebis, as well as chamchams[†] from an alley in Shikdarpara. Pupe Didi asks him where he lives; he replies, down Question Mark Lane in Whichtown.

Why don't I disclose his name? Because if I do, he'll be reduced to that name and that name only. There's only one 'I' and only one 'you' in this world; everybody else is 'he' or 'she'. The 'He' of my stories stands surety for all of them.

Let me tell you something else about him, otherwise I'll be to blame. Those who judge him only from my stories form a wrong impression about him. Those who have met him know that he's a handsome man with a serious expression. Like the night sky lit up by stars, his solemnity is lit up by hidden laughter. He's a first-rate person, really. No silly jokes and pranks can hurt him. It amuses me to show him up as a fool in my tales, for the simple reason that he's more intelligent than I am. He doesn't lose face even if he pretends to be stupid. This is helpful, because it makes for a link between Pupu's nature and his.

(*Se*, chapter 1)

THE HOLY MAN OF THE TREES

Udho: Did you find him?

Gobra: Now look here, Udho. Just because of something you said, I've been scouring all sorts of wild places for a month. I'm worn down to skin and bones, but I haven't yet spotted a hair of his head.

Panchu: Who is it you're looking for?

Gobra: The Holy Man of the Trees.

Panchu: The Holy Man of the Trees! Whoever is he?

Udho: Haven't you heard of him? The whole world knows who he is.

Panchu: Tell me about him.

Udho: Any tree that this Holy Man inhabits turns into a Wishing-Tree. You just stand under it and hold out your hand, and you get whatever you wish for.

Panchu: Who told you all this?

Udho: Bheku Sardar from Dhokar village. The
other day this Holy Man was sitting on a fig tree
and swinging his legs. Bheku, who didn't know
this, happened to be passing under the tree. He
was carrying a pot of thick treacle on his head to
blend with tobacco. The Holy Man's legs hit the
pot, and a stream of treacle ran down Bheku's face:
he couldn't even open his eyes or his mouth. The Holy Man is all
made of pity. 'Bheku,' he said, 'tell me your wish, and I'll let you
have it.' Bheku's a fool. He only said, 'Baba, give me a rag to clean
my face.' No sooner said but a towel came floating down from the
tree. When Bheku had wiped his face clean and looked up, there was
no one to be seen. You see, you can have only one wish and no more,
even if you bring the heavens down with your bawling.

Panchu: Oh dear, oh dear! No shawls, no fine clothes, just a towel!
What can you expect from a blockhead like Bheku?

Udho: But Bheku hasn't come badly out of this. Haven't you seen the
big shed he's built near Rathtala? It may have been just a towel, but it
was the Holy Man's blessed towel after all.

Panchu: Really? How did all this happen? By magic, was it?

Udho: Bheku went to the fair at Hondalpara and sat down with the towel
spread in front of him. Thousands of people flocked round him and
showered offerings on this towel to His Holiness: coins, vegetables, all
kinds of things. Women came to ask favours for their children: 'Bheku
Dada, please touch my son's head with the Baba's towel, he's been ailing
for three months now.' Bheku's fee for his divine services is five quarter-
rupees, five suparis,[†] five measures of rice and five dollops of ghee.[†]

Panchu: That's fine for Bheku, but do the devotees get anything in return?

Udho: Of course they do. Do you remember Gajan Pal? He filled
Bheku's towel with paddy for fifteen days in a row. He also tethered a
goat to one corner of the towel. The goat's bleating attracted more
people to Bheku. You won't believe me, but in eleven months flat
Gajan landed a job in the royal palace guard. His duties are to mix
drinks for the Chief of Police and comb and dress his whiskers.

Panchu: Is it really true?

Udho: Of course it's true. You know, I'm sort of related to Gajan: his wife's sister to the wife of a cousin of mine.

Panchu: Tell me, Udho, have you seen this towel yourself?

Udho: Of course I have. It's exactly like the stuff the Hatuganj weavers make: a yard and a half across, pale yellow like champak flowers, with a red border—just the same.

Panchu: Really? But how did this towel fall from the tree?

Udho: That's the miracle. All by the grace of the Holy Man.

Panchu: Let's go and find him. But how do we recognize him?

Udho: That's the problem. No one seems to have really seen him. And as ill luck would have it, that idiot Bheku's eyes were blinded by the treacle.

Panchu: What shall we do then?

Udho: Why, whenever I see anyone anywhere I join my hands and ask him, 'Please, sir, are you the Holy Man of the Trees?' This makes them turn very violent and abusive. One of them was so angry that he splashed the dirty water from his hookah[†] all over me.

Gobra: Never you mind, we shan't give up. We must find the Holy Man, and we may if we're lucky.

Panchu: Bheku says you can only see him when he's up on a tree, but not if he's down below.

Udho: You can't really put every man to test by asking him to climb a tree. But I'm trying out an idea. My amra tree is loaded with fruit, and I ask anyone I meet to climb up and help himself. All that's happened so far is that there's hardly any fruit left, and even the branches are broken.

Panchu: Now come along, we've no time to waste. If we're lucky we'll surely be able to find the Baba. Now let's call out together, 'O Holy Man of the Trees, dear Merciful Lord, where are you? If you're hiding somewhere among the parul creepers, do come out and show yourself to us poor creatures!'

Gobra: I say, something's stirring! It seems the Holy Man has listened to our prayers!

Panchu: Where? Where?

Gobra: On that chalta tree.

Panchu: What's there on the chalta tree? I can't see anything.

Gobra: Something's swinging there.

Panchu: That dangling thing? But it looks like a tail!

Udho: You're a dolt, Gobra. That's not our Holy Man: it's a monkey's tail. Can't you see it making faces at us?

Gobra: It's the sinful age[†] of the world. That's why the Holy Man has assumed the form of a monkey to elude us.

Panchu: You can't trick us, Holy Man: your black face[†] won't fool us. You can go on making faces as much as you wish, but we're not budging from here. Your holy tail will be our succour and protection.

Gobra: The Lord save us! The Holy Man's running away with enormous leaps!

Panchu: But where can he escape from us? We'll outrun him by the strength of our devotion.

Gobra: There now, he's climbed up the wood-apple tree.

Udho: Panchu, go up that tree.

Panchu: Why don't you go up?

Udho: I'm telling you to go up.

Panchu: No, no: I can't climb so high. Dear Holy Man, have mercy and come down to us!

Udho: Please, Holy Man, bless me that when it's time for me to leave this world, I may close my eyes with your holy tail round my neck.

(Se, chapter 3)

That Man dropped in while I was having my morning tea.

'Is there something you want to tell me?' I asked.

'Yes, there is,' he said.

Then please be sharp about it. I've got to go out right now.'

'Where to?'

'To the Governor's house.'

'Does the Governor often send for you?'

'No, he doesn't. It would have been better for him if he had.'

'Better? How?'

'He'd have known then that I'm far and away better at making up stories than his agents who're supposed to keep him informed. No one, not even a Rai Bahadur,[†] can match me in this. You know that, don't you?'

'Yes, I do, but what's all this rubbish you're making up about me these days?'

'I've been asked for fantastic stories.'

'Maybe so, but even fantastic stories must follow some pattern. Not crazy drivel that anybody can cook up.'

'Really? Let's have a sample of what you mean by a fantastic story.'

'All right. Just listen to me.'

While keeping goal for Mohan Bagan Club in a football fixture against Calcutta Club, Smritiratna[†] Mashai let in five goals, one after another. Swallowing so many goals didn't spoil his appetite: on the contrary, he grew ravenously hungry. The Ochterloney Monument[†] was near at hand; our goalkeeper started to lick it from the bottom up, all the way to the top. Badaruddin Mian, who was mending shoes in the Senate Hall,[†] rushed up at full speed and cried, 'You're such a learned man, so well versed in the scriptures! How could you defile this huge thing with your licks? Shameful, shameful,' he muttered, spat three times on the Monument, and headed for the office of *The Statesman*[†] newspaper to report the matter.

It suddenly struck Smritiratna Mashai that he had polluted his tongue. He walked across to the watchman at the Museum. 'Pandey Ji,' he said to the watchman, 'you're a brahman, so am I. You must help me.'

Pandey Ji saluted him and said, fingering his beard, *'Comment vous portez-vous, s'il vous plaît?'*[†]

Our scholar pondered for a while and said, 'A very baffling conundrum. I need to look into the books of Sankhya philosophy.[†] I'll give you my answer tomorrow. Not today, as I've polluted my tongue by licking the Monument.'

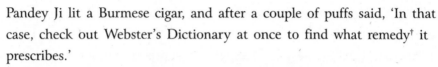

Pandey Ji lit a Burmese cigar, and after a couple of puffs said, 'In that case, check out Webster's Dictionary at once to find what remedy[†] it prescribes.'

Smritiratna said, 'Then I'll have to visit Bhatpara;[†] but that can wait. For the moment, lend me your brass-knobbed stick.'

'Why, what'll you do with it?' asked Pandey Ji. 'Have you got coal dust in your eyes?'

'How did you know that?' asked Smritiratna. 'It happened the day before yesterday. I had to run all the way to Ultadanga to see Dr McCartney, the well-known specialist of liver disorders. He arranged for a crowbar from Narkeldanga, and cleaned my eyes with it.'

'Then what do you want with my stick?' asked Pandey Ji.

'To use as a twig toothbrush.'[†]

'I see,' said Pandey Ji. 'I thought you might be wanting to tickle your nose to force out a sneeze. Had you done so, my stick would have had to be purified by washing it in Ganga water.'

That Man stopped here, pulled my hubble-bubble nearer him, and after a couple of draws on it, said, 'You see, Dada, this is a sample of your style of spinning yarns. Instead of using your own fingers to write, you seem to wield the trunk of the elephant-god Ganesh[†] to scribble your tall tales. You just twist facts, which is easy to do. Supposing you went about telling people that our Governor, after a stint as an oil merchant, has now set up a shop in Bagbazar to sell dried fish, who do you think would laugh at such a cheap joke? Is it worth your while to tickle the fancies of silly people?'

'You seemed peeved.'

'And with good reason. Only the other day you were telling Pupu Didi all kinds of rubbish about me, and she, being just a child, was hearing you open-mouthed. Don't forget, even weird stories need to be made up with some art.'

'Wasn't there any art in my story?'

'Absolutely none. I wouldn't have said a word if you hadn't dragged me into the matter. Suppose you'd said that you'd been entertaining your friends with curried giraffe brain, whalemeat fried with ground mustard, and pilau of hippos freshly caught from the river slime, with a dish of drumsticks made from the trunks of palm trees, I'd have said it was too crude. It's not at all difficult to write such things.'

'Is that so? Then let's have a specimen of your style instead.'

'Fair enough, but I hope you won't be cross. Dada, it's not that I'm more gifted than you: rather the opposite, but that's actually an advantage. Here's what I'd have said:

I was invited to Cardiff for a game of cards.† The head of the family there was a gentleman named Kojumachuku. His wife was Mrs Hachiendani Korunkuna. Their elder daughter, Pamkuni Devi by name, cooked with her own hands their celebrated dish, meriunathu of kintinabu, whose aroma wafts across seven districts. Its fragrance is so strong that it tempts even wild jackals to come out during the day and howl, whether out of greed or frustration I don't know; and the crows desperately flap their wings for three hours with their beaks stuck in the ground. And this was just a vegetable side-dish. Along with that came barrels of sangchani made of kangchuto, with the pulp of their delectable fruit anksuto dunked in it. The pudding was victimai of iktikuti—baskets of it. Before this was served, tame elephants were brought in to crush it under their feet. Then the largest of their beasts,

a cross between a man, a cow and a lion which they call gandisangdung, made it somewhat more tender by licking it with their sharp spiky tongues. And finally, before the three hundred places set for the diners, there arose the noise of huge mortars and pestles. The people there say this very din makes their mouths water, and attracts beggars from far and wide. Many lose their teeth while eating this food, and then they make a gift of their broken teeth to their host. The hosts

deposit these teeth in the bank and bequeath them to their children. The more teeth a person collects, the higher is his standing. Many people secretly buy other's collections and pass them off as their own. This has been a cause of many celebrated lawsuits. Lords of a thousand teeth are so high and mighty that they won't marry their daughters to families with only fifty teeth. A man with no more than fifteen teeth choked to death while eating a ketku sweet, and not a soul could be found in that quarter of the thousand-tooth tycoons who'd agree to take the body to be cremated. In the end the poor dead man was secretly floated down the Chowchangi River. This created a great uproar among people on both banks of the river. They sued for compensation, and the case went all the way up to the Privy Council.[†]

By this time I was gasping for breath. I said, 'Will you please stop and tell me what's so special about your story?'
'Just this: it's not a cheap chutney. It's no great crime if we amuse ourselves by embroidering matters about which we know nothing. Not that I claim my story has any superior humour about it. A bizarre story[†] becomes exciting only if you can make incredible things credible. Let me warn you, you'll land in disgrace if you keep on making up cheap popular pufferies that only take in children.'
'Fine,' I said. 'From now on I'll write stories so utterly credible that Pupu Didi will need a witch-doctor to exorcize her faith in them.'
'By the way, what did you mean when you said you were in a hurry to go to the Governor's house?'
'I meant that I can be free if you leave. Once you arrive, you simply stay put. I was just telling you in a roundabout way—go away!'
'Oh, I see. In that case, I'll go.'

(*Se*, chapter 5)

I was sitting one evening on the south terrace of my
house, facing a bank of ancient rain-trees that shut out
the stars; but they were lit up by fireflies, as though they
were winking at me out of a hundred eyes.

Pupe Didi was with me. I said to her, 'You've grown too
clever these days. I think I need to remind you that you
were once a little child.'

Pupe Didi laughed and retorted, 'That's where you score
over me. You must once have been a little child yourself,
but there's no way I can remind you of that.'

I sighed deeply and said, 'I don't think there's anyone left
who can do so. Yes, I too was a child once, but the only
witness to that are those stars in the sky. But let's not
talk about me. I was going to tell you about something
that happened when you were a child. You may or may
not like it, but it'll give me some pleasure to tell it.'

'Then go ahead.'

I think it was in early spring. For the past few days, you had been
listening avidly to the story of the Ramayana from shiny-pated
Kishori Chatto.[†] One morning, as I was reading the newspaper and
sipping my tea, you rushed in with startled eyes.

'What's the matter?' I asked.

You said breathlessly, 'I've been stolen away.'

'What a disaster! Who did this foul deed?'

You hadn't yet worked that out. You could easily have said 'Ravana',[†] but
you knew that wouldn't be true. Hadn't Ravana died only last evening
in battle, when not a single one of his ten heads was spared? So you
fumbled and faltered, and then said, 'He's asked me not to tell anyone.'

'That makes it more difficult. How can I rescue you then? Do you
know what direction he took?'

'He took me to a new country.'

'Was it Khandesh?'

'No.'

'Bundelkhand then?'

'No.'

'What sort of country was it?'

'It had rivers and hills, and great big trees. It was sometimes light and sometimes dark there.'

'But most countries are like that. Did you see some kind of demon, with his sharp spiky tongue hanging out?'

'Yes, yes, I did. He put out his tongue just once and vanished immediately.'

'Lucky for him, otherwise I'd have caught him by the scruff of his neck. Anyway, the person who stole you away must have taken you away in something. Was it in a chariot?'

'No.'

'On horseback?'

'No.'

'On top of an elephant?'

Suddenly you blurted out, 'On the back of a rabbit.'

That animal was much on your mind at the time because your father had just given you a pair on your birthday.

I said, 'Now I know who stole you away.'

'Tell me,' you said with a little smile.

'None other than Uncle Moon, I'm sure.'

'How do you know?'

'Because Uncle Moon has been a rabbit fancier[†] for a long, long time.'

'Where did he find his rabbits?'

'Not from your father.'

'Then from whom?'

'He stole them from Brahma's zoo.'[†]

'How disgraceful.'

'Disgraceful it was. That's why Brahma branded the Moon with black spots.'

'Serve him right.'

'But did he learn his lesson? Didn't he steal you as well? Perhaps he needed you to feed his rabbits with cauliflower leaves.'

This pleased you very much, and to test me you asked, 'Tell me: how could a rabbit carry me on its back?'

'Because you must have fallen asleep.'

'Does a person weigh less when she's asleep?'

'Yes, of course. Haven't you ever flown in your sleep?'

'Yes, of course I have.'

'Then where's the difficulty? Why a rabbit—even a toad could have carried you on its back and leapfrogged all over the field.'

'No, no, not a toad. How disgusting!'

'Don't worry, there aren't any toads on the moon. By the way, did you meet the Bangama bird[†] on your way?'

'Indeed I did.'

'And how did your meeting go?'

'He flew down from the top of a tamarisk tree and stood very tall. He thundered, 'Who's that running away with Pupe Didi?' As soon as the rabbit heard him, he ran away so fast that Bangama Dada couldn't catch up with him. What happened after that?'

'After what?'

'After the rabbit ran away with me.'

'How should I know? It's for you to tell me.'

'Really, how should I know? Didn't I fall asleep?'

'That's just the problem. That's why I can't trace where the rabbit took you—so I don't know which way I should go to rescue you.

Tell me, did you hear any bells ringing when you were being carried away?'

'Yes, yes, I did—ding-dong, ding-dong.'

'Then he must have taken you through the land of the Bell-Ears.'

'The Bell-Ears! Who are they?'

'They have two bells for ears, and two tails that end in two hammers. They beat on their ears with their tails— now one ear, then the other. There are two Bell-Eared tribes. One tribe is rather violent and has a shrill ring to their bells, the other is dignified and gives out deep sonorous rings.'

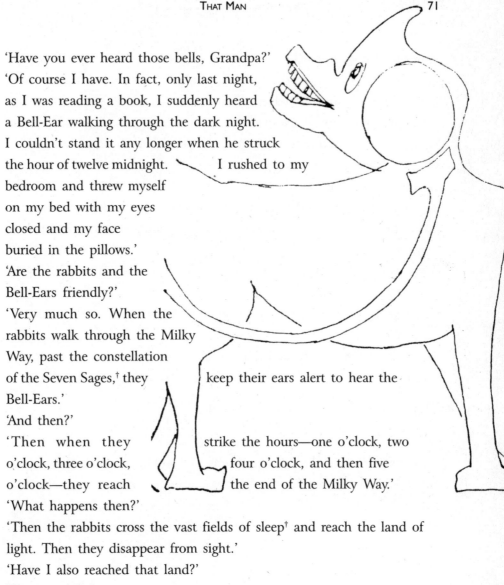

'Have you ever heard those bells, Grandpa?'
'Of course I have. In fact, only last night,
as I was reading a book, I suddenly heard
a Bell-Ear walking through the dark night.
I couldn't stand it any longer when he struck
the hour of twelve midnight.   I rushed to my
bedroom and threw myself
on my bed with my eyes
closed and my face
buried in the pillows.'
'Are the rabbits and the
Bell-Ears friendly?'
'Very much so. When the
rabbits walk through the Milky
Way, past the constellation
of the Seven Sages,[†] they   keep their ears alert to hear the
Bell-Ears.'
'And then?'
'Then when they   strike the hours—one o'clock, two
o'clock, three o'clock,   four o'clock, and then five
o'clock—they reach   the end of the Milky Way.'
'What happens then?'
'Then the rabbits cross the vast fields of sleep[†] and reach the land of
light. Then they disappear from sight.'
'Have I also reached that land?'
'Yes, certainly.'
'Then I'm no longer on the rabbit's back?'
'If you'd been, you'd have broken its back.'
'Yes, indeed. I forgot that I'm heavier now. So now what?'
'Now we must make plans to rescue you.'
'Of course you must. But how?'
'That's what's worrying me. I must take the help of a prince.'
'Where will you find a prince?'
'Well, I was thinking of Sukumar.'

Your face turned very grave as soon as I mentioned Sukumar. You said rather stiffly, 'I know you're fond of him because he takes lessons from you. That's why he's ahead of me in maths.'

There are other simple reasons for Sukumar being ahead, but I thought it better not to bring up the subject. I said, 'It's not a question of whether I like him or not; he's the only prince on call.'

'How do you know he's a prince?'

'He's reached an understanding with me to become Prince Permanent.'

You frowned and said, 'All his understanding seems to be only with you.'

'How can I help it? He doesn't listen to me because I'm so much older than him.'

'You call him a prince? I can't even think of him as the Jatayu Bird.[†] Humph!'

'Calm down now. We're in serious trouble. We don't even know where you are. Just this once, let him help us find you. Afterwards I'll turn him into a squirrel to help build Rama's bridge to Lanka.'[†]

'Why should he agree to help you? He's busy studying for his exam.'

Well, I'm three-quarters sure he'll agree. I saw him two days ago—last Saturday, around three o'clock in the afternoon. I had gone to visit his folk. I tracked him to the roof of their house: he was walking about there, having managed to slip away from his mother's watchful eyes. 'What's going on?' I asked him.

He tossed his head and announced, 'I'm a prince.'

'Where's your sword?'

He showed me a half-burnt stick, left over from a rocket lit on Diwali night, which he'd fastened to his waist with a string.

'Yes, I see you have a sword; but you need a horse.'

'There's one in the stable.'

He ran to a corner of the roof and fetched an old broken umbrella, thrown away by his uncle. He tucked the umbrella between his legs, and with a shout of 'Gee-ho gee-up', he ran round the roof.

'Truly a marvellous horse,' I agreed.

'Do you want to see him with his wings?'

'I certainly do.'

He unfurled the umbrella. Some grains of horsefeed fell out from it.

'A marvel, a marvel!' I cried. 'I never thought I'd live to see a winged horse.'

'Now, Grandpa, I'm flying off. Close your eyes, and you'll see that I've reached the clouds. It's very dark there.'

'I don't have to close my eyes. I can see you quite clearly—flying very fast, and the wings of your horse have disappeared behind the clouds.'

'Grandpa, can you suggest a name for my horse?'

'Chhatrapati,'† I said.

He liked the name. He patted the umbrella on the back and shouted, 'Chhatrapati!'

Then, acting the part of the horse, he replied, 'Yes, sir!'

He looked at me and asked, 'Did you think I said "Yes, sir"? Not at all, it was the horse.'

'You don't have to tell me. I'm not so deaf.'

The prince said to the horse, 'Chhatrapati, I don't like sitting here quietly.'

The horse replied, 'Tell me your command.'

'Let's cross the fields of Tepantar.'

'Yes, let's.'

I couldn't stay any longer. I had other things to do. I had to break up the party and say, 'Prince, I believe I saw your teacher waiting for you. He didn't seem to be in a very good mood.'

The prince grew very restless at this. He prodded the umbrella and said, 'Can't you fly me somewhere at once?'

I had to speak for the poor horse. 'He can't fly until it's night. During the day he pretends to be an umbrella, but as soon as you fall asleep at night he'll spread his wings. It's better for you to go down to your teacher now, otherwise you'll be in trouble.'

As he went down, Sukumar said, 'But I haven't finished all I had to say.'

'You can never finish all you have to say,' I answered. 'If it were to finish, there would be no fun left.'

'My lessons will be over by five o'clock, Grandpa. You must come back after that.'

'You mean that you'll have done with your Grade Three Reader. You'll need a change to a grade-one story. All right, I promise I'll come.'

(Se, chapter 10)

Next morning, Pupe Didi brought the breakfast I'd ordered: sprouted chickpeas and molasses in a stoneware bowl. I've set about reviving ancient Bengali food culture in this modern age.

'Would you like some tea?' Pupe Didi asked me.

'No, some date palm juice,' I replied.

She said, 'You look rather strange. Did you have any bad dreams?'

'Shadows of dreams flicker through my mind all the time,' I said.

'Then the dreams dissolve and the shadows pass as well, leaving no trace. But today I want to tell you something about your childhood that keeps coming back to me.'

'Why don't you?'

'One day I'd put down my pen and was sitting on my balcony. You were there, and so was Sukumar. It grew dark: they lit the street lamps. I was telling you, making up most of it, about Satya Yuga,† the Age of Truth—ages and ages ago.'

'Making it up, were you? You mean you were turning the Age of Truth into the Age of Lies!'

'Don't call it lies. Just because the ultra-violet ray can't be seen, it doesn't mean that it's unreal—it's a genuine kind of light. The Age of Truth existed in the Ultra-Violet Age of human history. I wouldn't call it prehistoric but ultra-historic.'

'Spare me your explanations and tell me what you were going to say.'

'I was trying to impress upon you that in the Age of Truth people didn't learn from books or from the news they heard. Their knowledge came from Being.'

'I can't follow you at all.'

'Then listen to me carefully. You believe you know me well, don't you?'

'Yes, very well.'

'And so you do; but that knowledge leaves ninety-nine per cent of me out of account. If in your heart of hearts you could have turned yourself into me whenever you wished, then you'd really have known me.'

'Are you telling me we know nothing?'

'Indeed we don't. But we've all agreed to think we know, and all our relations are on that basis.'

'But we seem to be getting along quite well.'

'Maybe, but it wasn't like that in the Age of Truth. That's what I was telling you. In those days there was no Knowing by Seeing or Knowing by Touching, only Knowing by Being.'

Women's minds take hold of concrete things, so I thought Pupu would find my words quite unreal—she wouldn't like it at all. But she seemed interested and said, 'What fun!'

She then went on excitedly, 'Now, Grandpa, they say science these days is playing all kinds of tricks. You can listen to songs sung by someone who's dead, you can see a person who's far away; they say they're even turning lead into gold. Perhaps some day one person will just be able to pass into another by some sort of electrical trick.'

'Quite possibly, but then what would you do? Because then you wouldn't be able to hide anything.'

'Goodness! Everyone has a lot of things to hide.'

'They've got something to hide because they keep it hidden. If nobody hid anything, if it were all like an open card game where you could see what cards everybody held, people would deal with each other on that basis.'

'But people have a lot of shameful things to keep to themselves.'

'If the shameful things about everybody were known, we wouldn't feel so ashamed.'

'Never mind all that. What were you going to say about me?'

'I asked you that day how you'd have liked to see yourself if you'd been born during the Age of Truth, and you promptly said, "As an Afghan cat".'

Pupe was furious. She said, 'I never said anything of the sort. You're making it up.'

'I might make up stories about the Age of Truth, but what you said was all your own. Even a wordsmith like me couldn't have made that up instantly.'

'And I suppose it made you think I'm very silly.'

'No, not at all. I only deduced that you badly wanted an Afghan cat but had no means of getting one, as your father loathes cats. In my view, in the Age of Truth no one would need to buy a cat or get one as a gift; but if you so wished, you could change yourself into a cat.'

'What use would it be to change from a human being into a cat? It's better to buy one: if you can't buy one, it's best not to have one at all.'

'There you are. You can't imagine the glory of the Age of Truth. In that age, Pupe could easily extend her frontiers to include a cat; but she wouldn't wipe out her own frontiers. You'd be both yourself and the cat.'

'What you're saying makes no sense at all.'

'It makes perfect sense in terms of the Age of Truth. Don't you remember how the other day you heard your teacher Pramatha Babu say that light descends in particles like raindrops, but also flows in waves like a stream? Our ordinary sense tells us it must be either one or the other, but science says it's both at the same time. So you too could be at once Pupu and a cat. That's what the Age of Truth is all about.'

'The older you grow, Grandpa, the harder it gets to understand what you say—just like your poetry.'

'Obviously it's a sign that I'll grow quite silent one day.'

'Didn't our conversation get beyond the Afghan cat that day?'

Indeed it did. Sukumar, who had been sitting quietly in a corner, suddenly burst into speech as if he were dreaming: 'I want to see what it's like to be a sal tree.'

You, Pupe, have always looked for a chance to make Sukumar look foolish. You were in stitches when he said he wanted to be a sal tree. The poor boy was very embarrassed. So I took his side and said, 'The wind starts blowing from the south, the branches break out in flowers, an invisible current of magic runs through the heart of the tree and bursts out in a splendid show of beauty and scent. Of course you want to sense this wonderful feeling rising up from inside you. If you don't become a tree, how can you feel the endless thrill of a tree in springtime?'

Perhaps inspired by what I said, Sukumar cried excitedly, 'I can see a sal tree from my bedroom window. When I lie down on my bed I can see its top. It seems to be dreaming.'

When you heard Sukumar talking about a dreaming sal tree, you were perhaps about to say, 'How silly!' But I stepped in and said, 'The whole existence of a sal tree is a dream. It's in a dream that it passes from a seed to a shoot, from a shoot to a tree. The leaves are its dream-talk.'

I asked Sukumar, 'That morning when it was raining heavily from a cloudy sky I saw you standing quietly on the north balcony, clutching the railings. What were you thinking about?'

Sukumar said, 'I don't know what I was thinking about.'

I said, 'These unknown thoughts of yours filled your mind, just as the sky had filled with clouds. When trees stand still, they too are full of unknown feelings. Those unknown thoughts deepen in the shadow of monsoon clouds and sparkle in the winter morning sun. The same unknown thoughts make them murmur through the young leaves and sing through the flower-buds.'

I still remember how Sukumar's eyes grew wide at this. He said, 'If I were a tree, that murmur would climb up my body towards the clouds in the sky.'

You realized that Sukumar was getting too much attention, so you brushed him aside and took the stage. You asked me, 'Grandpa, if the Age of Truth returns, what would you like to be?'

I knew you were expecting me to say that I wanted to be a mastodon or a megatherium, because we'd been talking a few days earlier about creatures in the first chapter of the book of life. The world was young then, its bones still delicate; its landmasses hadn't firmed up, its trees looked like the first uncertain brush-strokes of the Creator. I had told you that human beings today have no clear idea how those huge behemoths lived in that primeval forest in the unstable climate of those times. From what I'd said, you'd sensed an urge to find out about those early days of life's adventure, like the age of the old epic heroes. I'm sure you'd have been pleased if I'd said I wanted to be a primitive hairy four-tusked elephant. It would have been within striking distance of your wish to be an Afghan cat, so you'd have had me on your side. I could have said something like that, but talking to Sukumar had made me think of other things.

I wanted to become a scene, spread over a wide stretch of ground—in the first hour of morning, towards the end of the winter month of Magh. The wind would have risen, making the old banyan tree turn restless as a child, the river break out in sound, and the band of trees along the uneven riverbank grow blurred. Beyond all this there would be the open sky, and in it a sense of distant space—as though the sound of a bell were being wafted on the wind in the faintest possible way across a great expanse, infusing the sunshine with its message: the day's at end.

From your expression, you clearly thought it was much more wayward to imagine oneself as a whole landscape—river, forest and sky—than as a single tree.

But Sukumar said, 'It's rather fun to think of you as spread across everything—the river, the trees. Tell me: will the Age of Truth ever come back?'

'Until it does, we have pictures and poems. They're the best way to forget about oneself and turn into something else.'

'Have you drawn a picture of the scene you're talking about?' asked Sukumar.

'Yes, I have.'

'I'll draw one too.'

On hearing Sukumar speak so boldly, you burst out: 'What makes you think you'll be able to?'

'Of course he will,' I said. 'And when you've finished, I'll have your picture, and you can have mine.'

That's as far as our conversation went that day.

(*Se*, chapter 14)

The Welcome

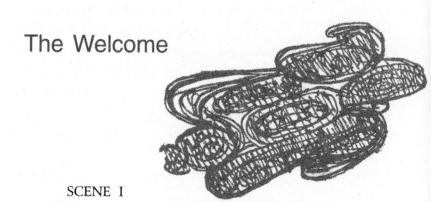

SCENE I

[A village road.
Chaturbhuj Babu has come back to the village after passing his MA
examinations, hoping that everyone will make a great fuss over him. There is a
plump Afghan cat with him.
Enter Nilratan.]

Nilratan: Hello there, Chatu Babu. When did you arrive?

Chaturbhuj: Directly after the MA exams were over. I—

Nilratan: Ah, you've got a fine cat there!

Chaturbhuj: This year the exams were very—

Nilratan: Tell me, where did you find that cat?

Chaturbhuj: Bought it. The subjects I'd offered—

Nilratan: How much did you pay for it?

Chaturbhuj: I don't remember. Nilratan Babu, has anybody passed any exams in our village?

Nilratan: Oh, lots of them. But you won't see a cat like that in these parts.

Chaturbhuj: (*to himself*) Confound him, he can't talk about anything but cats—it doesn't seem to matter that I've just passed my MA!

[*Enter the Zamindar.*†]

Zamindar: Ah, Chaturbhuj—what have you been doing in Calcutta all this time?

Chaturbhuj: I've just finished my MA, sir.

Zamindar: Finished off your daughter?† Your own *meye*! How could you do it?

Chaturbhuj: You've got me wrong—after passing the BA I—

Zamindar: Married her off! And we didn't get to hear of it?

Chaturbhuj: Not a marriage†—a BA—

Zamindar: Oh, it's all the same—what you city people call a BA, we call a *biye*† in these backwaters. Anyway, let it pass—this cat of yours is a stunner, I must say.

Chaturbhuj: You're mistaken, sir, my—

Zamindar: No mistake about it. You won't find another such cat in the whole district!

Chaturbhuj: But we're not discussing cats!

Zamindar: Of course we are—I'm telling you you won't find another cat like this!

Chaturbhuj: (*to himself*) Confound him!

Zamindar: Why don't you drop by my place with your cat sometime this evening? The boys would be delighted.

Chaturbhuj: Of course—I quite understand. They haven't seen me for a long time.

Zamindar: Yes, I suppose so…but what I mean is, even if you can't come yourself, send Beni round with the cat—I want the boys to see it. (*Exit*)

[*Enter Uncle Satu.*]

Satu: How are you, my boy? Been away a long time, haven't you?

Chaturbhuj: That's right. There were so many examinations—

Satu: This cat of yours—

Chaturbhuj: (*furiously*) I'm going home. (*About to leave*)

Satu: Hey, wait a minute—this cat—

Chaturbhuj: No, sir, I've got work to do.

Satu: Oh come on, now, answer a civil question. This cat—(*Chaturbhuj strides away without another word*) Just look at that. It's education that's ruining these young people. We know what they're worth, but they're stuffed full of conceit!

SCENE II

[*Inside Chaturbhuj's house.*]

Maid: Mother, Dada Babu has come home in a blazing temper.

Mother: Why, what's the matter?

Maid: I don't know.

[*Enter Chaturbhuj.*]

Little Boy: Dada, can I have this cat?

Chaturbhuj: (*slaps him hard*) Cat, cat, cat the whole day long, is it?

Mother: No wonder the poor boy's angry! He comes home after such a long time and these brats start annoying him at once.—(*To Chaturbhuj*) Let me have the cat, son. I'll give it some rice and milk that I've put by.

Chaturbhuj: (*furiously*) Here, mother, you can have the cat and feed it all you want. I shan't stop to eat—I'm leaving at once.

Mother: (*plaintively*) What makes you say such a thing?—Your meal's ready and waiting, dear. You can sit down to it as soon as you've had your bath!

Chaturbhuj: No, I'm leaving. You're all crazy about cats in these parts. No one cares for men of worth. (*Kicks out at the cat*)

Aunt: Don't hurt the cat—she hasn't done any harm.

Chaturbhuj: When it comes to a cat you're all heart, but you have no pity for human beings! (*Exit*)

Little Girl: (*looking out*) Come and see, Uncle Hari—what a big fat tail!
Hari: Whose tail—Chaturbhuj's?
Girl: No, the cat's.

SCENE III

[*On the road.*
Enter Chaturbhuj, bag in hand, without the cat.] ·

Sadhucharan: Sir, where's that cat of yours?
Chaturbhuj: It's dead.
Sadhucharan: How sad! How did it happen?
Chaturbhuj: (*irritably*) I don't know!

[*Enter Paran Babu.*]

Paran: Hello! What's happened to your cat?
Chaturbhuj: It's dead.
Paran: No, really! How?
Chaturbhuj: The same way all of you'll die—by swinging at the end of a rope!
Paran: Good God, he's positively furious!

[*A swarm of urchins run after Chaturbhuj, clapping and teasing him with cries of 'Pussy cat, pussy cat!'*]

Curtain

The Poet and the Pauper

[*Enter Kunjabihari Babu, the celebrated poet, and Bashambad Babu.*[†]]

Kunja: What brings you here, my good man?

Bashambad: Sir, I'm starving. You'd talked about a job...

Kunja: (*interrupting hurriedly*) A job? Work? Who thinks of work in this sweet autumn weather?

Bashambad: No one does so of choice, sir; it's this hunger that—

Kunja: Hunger? Fie, fie, what a mean, paltry word! Pray do not repeat it before me!

Bashambad: Very good sir, I won't. But I can't help thinking about it all the time.

Kunja: Really, Bashambad Babu! All the time? Even on a serene, tranquil, beautiful evening such as this?

Bashambad: Yes indeed. I'm thinking even more about it now than I usually do. I had a little rice at half-past ten before I set out job-hunting, and I haven't had a bite since then.

Kunja: Does it matter? Must you eat? (*Bashambad scratches his head in silence.*) Doesn't one wish, sitting in this autumn moonlight, that a man might live without gorging himself like a beast? That these moonbeams,

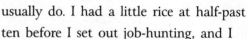

the nectar of flowers and the spring breeze might suffice for all his needs?

Bashambad: (*terrified, softly*) Sir, that would hardly suffice to hold body and soul together—one needs something more substantial to eat.

Kunja: (*heatedly*) Then go away and eat! Go stuff yourself with gobbets of rice and dal† and curry! This is no place for you—you're trespassing.

Bashambad: I'll go at once, sir. Just tell me where I might find that rice and dal and curry! (*Seeing that Kunja Babu looks very angry*) No, Kunja Babu, you're quite right: the breeze from your garden is enough to fill one's belly, one doesn't really need anything else.

Kunja: I'm glad to hear you say so—spoken like a man! Well, let's go outside, then. Why stay indoors when there's such a lovely garden to walk in?

Bashambad: Yes, let's. (*Softly, to himself*) There's a chill in the air, and I don't even have a wrap…

Kunja: Wonderful! How charming autumn is!

Bashambad: That's right—but a little cold, don't you think?

Kunja: (*wrapping his shawl closely around himself*) Cold? Not at all.

Bashambad: No, no, not at all! (*His teeth chatter.*)

Kunja: (*looking up at the sky*) What a sight to gladden the eye! Fleecy puffs of cloud sailing like proud swans in the azure lake, and amidst them the moon, like—

Bashambad: (*has a violent fit of coughing*) Ahem, ahem, ahem!

Kunja: …the moon, like—

Bashambad: Cough, cough—ahem!

Kunja: (*nudging him roughly*) Do you hear me, Bashambad Babu? The moon, like—

Bashambad: Wait a minute—ah, ah, ahem, cough, cough!

Kunja: (*losing his temper*) What sort of philistine are you, sir? If you must go on wheezing like this, you should wrap yourself in a blanket and huddle in a corner of your room. In such a garden…

Bashambad: (*frightened, desperately suppressing another cough*) But I have nothing—(*aside*) neither a blanket nor a wrap!

Kunja: This delightful ambience reminds me of a song. Let me sing it.

> *This bea-oo-tiful gro-o-ve, these bloo-oo-ming trees,*
> *The winsome bakul—*

Bashambad: (*sneezes thunderously*) Ah - h - choo!

Kunja: *The winsome bakul—*

Bashambad: Ahchoo! Ahchoo!

Kunja: D'you hear? *The winsome bakul—*

Bashambad: Ahchoo! Ahchoo!

Kunja: Get out. Get out of my garden!

Bashambad: Just a minute—ahchoo!

Kunja: Get out at once, you…

Bashambad: I'm going, I'm going, I don't want to stay here a moment longer. If I don't leave at once my life will take leave of me—ahchoo! The liquid sweetness of autumn is overflowing through my nose and eyes—I'll sneeze my life out in a moment—ahchoo! ahchoo! Cough, cough, cough… But Kunja Babu, about that job—ahchoo! (*Exit*)

[*Kunja Babu draws his shawl closer and gazes silently at the moon. Enter Servant.*]

Servant: Dinner is served.

Kunja: Why so late? Does it take two hours to get the food ready? (*Hurries out*)

Curtain

The Ordeals of Fame

SCENE I

[*Dukari Datta, lawyer, seated on a chair. Enter Kangalicharan—timidly, subscription book in hand.*]

Dukari: What do you want?

Kangali: Sir, you're a patriot—

Dukari: Everybody knows that, but what brings you here?

Kangali: For the public good, you have been trying with might and main—

Dukari: —to make a living out of lawsuits; that's common knowledge too. What have you got to say?

Kangali: Sir, it's nothing much, really.

Dukari: Well then, why don't you get it over?

Kangali: If you think a little you will have to agree that *Ganat parataram nahi*†—

Dukari: Look here, I can't think or agree about anything until I know what it means! Translate that into Bengali.

Kangali: I'm not sure what it would be in Bengali, but what it means is that music is delightful to hear.

Dukari: Not to everybody.

Kangali: He who doesn't like music is—

Dukari: —the lawyer Dukari Datta.

Kangali: Don't say such a thing, sir.

Dukari: Why not? Would you rather I lied?

Kangali: In ancient India the sage Bharata was the first great singer to—

Dukari: Is there a lawsuit involving him? Otherwise cut your lecture short.

Kangali: I had a lot of things to say—

Dukari: But I have no time to hear them.

Kangali: Then I shall be brief. In this great metropolis we have founded an organization called the Society for the Advancement of Music, and we'd like you, sir, to—

Dukari: Give a speech?

Kangali: Oh no!

Dukari: Preside over a function?

Kangali: Not at all.

Dukari: Then what is it you want me to do? I'm warning you, I can neither sing nor listen to people singing.

Kangali: Oh, rest assured, sir, you shan't have to do either. (*Advancing the subscription book*) Only a small donation—

Dukari: (*with a violent start*) Donation? O calamity! You're a very devious man—creeping in timidly in that harmless kind of way...I thought you might have got into a lawsuit. Get out this minute, and take that subscription book with you, else I'll file a police case for trespass!

Kangali. I came for a donation, and you're throwing me out!† (*Under his breath*) But just you wait—I'll fix you.

SCENE II

[*Enter Dukari Babu, newspapers in hand.*]

Dukari: Here's fun! Someone called Kangalicharan has told all the papers that I've donated five thousand rupees to the Society for the Advancement for Music. Donation be damned, I nearly thrust the man out by the neck! This is good publicity, though—it'll give my practice a boost. They'll gain something too—people will think it must be a really big organization if it can draw five-thousand-rupee gifts. They'll get fat subscriptions from all kinds of other places. Anyway, I'm a lucky man.

[*Enter Clerk.*]

Clerk: So you've donated five thousand rupees to the Society for the Advancement of Music, sir?
Dukari: (*scratching his head and smiling*) I—Oh, that's just something people are saying. Don't take it seriously. But suppose I have given it, why make a fuss?
Clerk: What modesty! First he gives away five thousand rupees, then hushes it up as a trifle—truly no ordinary man!

[*Enter Servant.*]

Servant: There's a crowd of people downstairs.
Dukari: (*to himself*) There you are! My custom's swelling already. (*Aloud, happily*) Call them up here one by one, and fetch some paan† and tobacco for them.

[*Enter First Visitor.*]

Dukari: (*pulling up a chair*) Come in, please. Have a smoke. Boy, get the gentleman some paan.
First Visitor: (*to himself*) What a charming personality! If he doesn't fulfil my heart's desire, who will?
Dukari: Well, sir, what brings you here?
First Visitor: Sir, your magnanimity is well-known through the land.
Dukari: Why do you listen to these rumours?
First Visitor: Such modesty! Sir, I'd only heard about your greatness, now my doubts have been laid at rest.
Dukari: (*to himself*) I wish he'd get to the point…there are a lot of people waiting. (*Aloud*) Ah, yes—so what can I do for you?
First Visitor: For the uplift of the nation the heart must—

Dukari: —That, of course, goes without saying—

First Visitor: True, true. Large-hearted gentlemen like yourself who, for the sake of India's—

Dukari: I admit everything, my dear sir; forget all that and proceed.

First Visitor: It's the sign of a modest man that when he hears himself praised—

Dukari: For God's sake, man, come to the point!

First Visitor: The fact is, our country's fortunes are declining day by day—

Dukari: —Only because we can't keep our speeches short.

First Visitor: India, our sacred motherland, engenderer of golden harvests, is floundering in the dark pit of penury...

Dukari: (*clutching his head in despair*) Go on.

First Visitor: —in the dark pit of penury, day by day—

Dukari: (*in a stricken voice*) I don't know what you're talking about!

First Visitor: Then let me come to the crux of the matter.

Dukari: (*eagerly*) That's much better.

First Visitor: The British are looting us.

Dukari: Fine—just get me the evidence. I'll file a suit in the magistrate's court.

First Visitor: The magistrate is looting too.

Dukari: Then in the district judge's court—

First Visitor: The district judge is a very brigand!

Dukari: (*startled*) I don't understand you at all.

First Visitor: The country's wealth is being shipped abroad.

Dukari: How sad.

First Visitor. Therefore, a public meeting—

Dukari: (*alarmed*) A meeting!

First Visitor: Here's the subscription book.

Dukari: (*gaping*) A subscription book!

First Visitor: A small donation—

Dukari: (*leaping off his seat*) Donation! Get out—get out—get out...

(*Upsets the chair, overturns a bottle of ink. First Visitor runs off, falls, rises again. Confusion.*)

[*Enter Second Visitor.*]

Dukari: What do you want?

Second Visitor: Sir, your well-known magnanimity—

Dukari: Enough, enough—I've heard that already…have you got anything new to say?

Second Visitor: Your profound concern for the country's welfare—

Dukari: Confound it, this fellow's saying just the same things!

Second Visitor: Your interest in all kinds of patriotic initiatives—

Dukari: Here's a nuisance! Just what is it you want?

Second Visitor: A meeting—

Dukari: Another meeting!

Second Visitor: Here's the book.

Dukari: Book! What book?

Second Visitor: The subscription book—

Dukari. Subscriptions? (*Dragging him up by the hand*) Get up, get up, get out—get out if you value your life—

[*The subscription-hunter flees without another word. Enter Third Visitor.*]

Dukari: Look here, I've heard everything about my patriotic spirit, my generosity, my modesty—all that's over. Start from after that.

Third Visitor: Your breadth of vision—cosmopolitanism—liberality—

Dukari: That's better, it sounds a bit different. But sir, let's dispense with all that too—start talking in plain prose, will you?

Third Visitor: We're thinking of a library—

Dukari: A library? You're sure it's not a meeting you mean?

Third Visitor: No sir, not a meeting.

Dukari: Thank heavens. A library—excellent! Carry on, carry on.

Third Visitor: Here's our prospectus.

Dukari: You don't have any other kind of book as well, do you?

Third Visitor: No sir, not a book, only some printed papers.

Dukari: I see. Go on.

Third Visitor: A small subscription, if you please.

Dukari: (*leaping to his feet*) Subscription? Help! My house has been attacked by robbers today. Police! Police!

[*Third Visitor flees in breathless haste. Enter Harashankar Babu.*]

Dukari: Is that Harashankar? Come in, come in! We haven't met since we left college—I can't tell you how glad I am to see you.

Harashankar: Yes, we must have a long chat some time, old friend—but later on. Let me dispose of a serious matter first.

Dukari: (*delighted*) I haven't heard of a serious matter for quite some time—go right ahead, it'll be music to my ears. (*Harashankar draws out a receipt-book from under his wrap.*) Good lord, another receipt-book!

Harashankar: The boys in our neighbourhood are planning a meeting—

Dukari: (*startled*) A meeting!

Harashankar: That's right, a meeting. So I've come for a small subscription—

Dukari: A subscription?—Look here, it's true we've been friends for a long time, but if you utter that word before me again we'll have to part company for ever. I'm warning you.

Harashankar: Is that so? You can squander five thousand rupees on some obscure Music Society in Khargachhia, but you can't sign up for five rupees to oblige an old friend! Only a shameless scoundrel would set foot in this house again.

[*Storms out of the room. Enter another Stranger, book in hand.*]

Dukari: Another of those infernal receipt-books! Get lost!

Stranger: (*scared*) But Nandalal Babu said—

Dukari: I don't want to hear about any Nandalal. Get out, I say!

Stranger: Sir, about the money—

Dukari: I won't give you a paisa. Get out!

[*The stranger flees.*]

Clerk: Sir, sir, what have you done? He came to pay the money Nandalal Babu owes you! We must have that money today at all costs.
Dukari: Good heavens! Call him back, call him back.

[*Exit Clerk. Re-enter presently.*]

Clerk: He's gone, I couldn't find him.
Dukari: Now here's a pretty mess.

[*Enter a man carrying a tanpura.*[†]]

Dukari: What brings you here?
Musician: Oh, sir, where shall I find such a connoisseur of the arts? What have you not done to encourage music! I've come to sing for you. (*Promptly starts strumming on his tanpura and singing in the yamankalyan raga.*)

      Of Dukari Datta is my ditty—
      The world has never seen the like of his charity...(*etc.*)

Dukari: Heavens, what a noise! Shut up, will you?

[*Enter another musician with tanpura.*]

Second Musician: What does *he* know about music? Listen to this—
      Dukari Datta, glory be—
      Who knows your greatness, if not me?
First Musician: Cha-a-a-ri-i-i-te-e-e-...
Second Musician: Du-u-k-a-a-ri-i-i...
First Musician: Du-u-ka-a-a...
Dukari: (*stopping his ears*) Help! For God's sake help!

[*A drummer walks in with a tabla set.*[†]]

Drummer: How can you sing without a beat?

[*Gets going at once. Enter Second Drummer.*]

Second Drummer: What does this fool know about accompaniment? He hasn't even learnt how to hold the drums properly.

First Drummer: Shut up, you rogue!

Second Drummer: Shut up yourself.

First Drummer: What do you know of music?

Second Drummer: What do you know about it?

[*The musicians argue furiously, and finally start beating each other. The drummers also argue, and start pitching their tablas at each other. Hordes of singers, players and subscription-hunters invade the room.*]

First: Sir, a song—

Second: Sir, a donation—

Third: Sir, a meeting—

Fourth: Your munificence—

Fifth: A khayal[†] in the yamankalyan raga—

Sixth: The country's welfare—

Seventh: Shori Miyan's[†] tappa[†]—

Eighth: Hey you, clam up for a second—

Ninth: Let me get a word in, will you?

[*They all start tugging at Dukari's clothes, everyone yelling 'Listen to me, sir', 'No, to me, sir—'.*]

Dukari: (*to the clerk, desperately*) I'm leaving for my uncle's place. I'll be away for some time. For God's sake don't give anyone the address!

[*Exit. The excited musicians fight among themselves. The clerk struggles to break them up until he drops down, battered, in the evening.*]

Curtain

My Childhood

I was born in the Calcutta of yesteryear. In those days horse-drawn
carriages still rattled through the streets, leaving a trail of dust, the
coachmen lashing the skinny horses with hempen whips. There were no
trams, no buses, no motor cars. People weren't always in such a
breathless hurry then; the days passed at a leisurely pace. The babus
left for their offices after a long smoke on their hookahs, chewing on a
wad of paan,[†] some in palanquins and some in shared hansom cabs.
Rich men had their own carriages painted with the family insignia,
draped with leather half-curtains; the coachman sat on the coach-box
with a turban perched on his head; two pairs of footmen rode at the
back with yak-tail fans tucked in their belts, startling pedestrians with
their sudden cries. Women were shy of riding in carriages; when they
went out it was always in the stuffy darkness of closed palanquins.
They never used umbrellas in rain or shine. A woman who wore a
chemise or shoes was mocked as a memsahib,[†] implying that she was a
shameless creature. If a woman accidentally met a man other than a close
relation, she would bite her tongue in embarrassment, turn
aside and draw down the end of her sari beyond her nose.
Their palanquins had closed doors, just like their rooms. When
women of rich families went out, the palanquins were draped in
thick curtains over and above the roof and sides, making them

look like moving tombs. A darwan[†] walked alongside, brass-bound
cudgel in hand. It was the darwan's duty to guard the front gate of the
house, stroking his beard; to take money to the bank and womenfolk
to their relatives' houses; and on festival days, to escort the master's
wife for a holy dip in the river Ganga, palanquin and all. When pedlars
came to the door with their boxes full of wares, they knew that
Shiunandan, the darwan, would take his cut. Then there were the
cabmen: if any of them thought that the darwan was asking for too
much cut-money, he would make a great row at the gate. Our sergeant-
at-gate, Shobharam, was a wrestler; every now and then he used to flex
his arms and swing heavy clubs around his head, or prepare a bowl of
siddhi,[†] or chomp raw radish, leaves and all, with great relish while we
yelled 'Radha-Krishna!' into his ear. The more he protested and threw
up his arms, the more lustily we shouted. He had hit upon this wile to
hear the names of the gods he worshipped.

There were neither gas lamps then nor electric lights; when the
first paraffin lamps arrived later on, we were amazed at their
brightness. A servant came in the evenings to light our castor-
oil lamps. In our study, there would be a double-wicked lamp.
By the flickering light of that lamp, our tutor[†] taught us from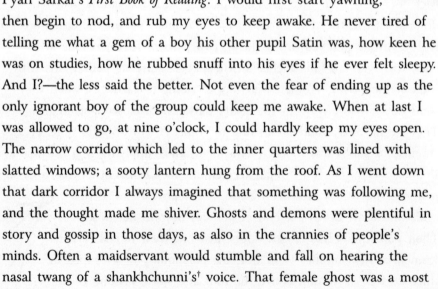
Pyari Sarkar's *First Book of Reading*. I would first start yawning,
then begin to nod, and rub my eyes to keep awake. He never tired of
telling me what a gem of a boy his other pupil Satin was, how keen he
was on studies, how he rubbed snuff into his eyes if he ever felt sleepy.
And I?—the less said the better. Not even the fear of ending up as the
only ignorant boy of the group could keep me awake. When at last I
was allowed to go, at nine o'clock, I could hardly keep my eyes open.
The narrow corridor which led to the inner quarters was lined with
slatted windows; a sooty lantern hung from the roof. As I went down
that dark corridor I always imagined that something was following me,
and the thought made me shiver. Ghosts and demons were plentiful in
story and gossip in those days, as also in the crannies of people's
minds. Often a maidservant would stumble and fall on hearing the
nasal twang of a shankhchunni's[†] voice. That female ghost was a most

ill-tempered thing, and she was a glutton for fish. There was a large leafy nut tree at the western corner of the house. Many people claimed to have seen a shape standing with one foot on the third-storey roof and another on a branch of that tree; there were also many people ready to believe it. When a friend of my elder brother's laughed at the story, the servants muttered darkly that he was a most irreligious man,

and all his learning would prove of no use when the evil spirit broke his neck. The air was so thick with dreadful superstitions that one's flesh crept if one stretched one's legs under the table.

We didn't have mains water either. In the months of Magh and Phalgun,[†] the water-carrier would sling a bamboo pole over his shoulder, hang pitchers from it, and fetch enough drinking water from the Ganga to last us the whole year through. All that water was stored in huge pitchers, row on row, in a dark room on the ground floor. Everybody knew that the creatures who lurked in those dark, damp cells had huge gaping mouths, eyes on their chests, and ears the size of winnowing-fans; their feet pointed backwards. My heart pounded whenever I walked past those eerie shadows towards our back garden, and I would hurry as fast as I could.

At high tide the Ganga water used to come rushing through brick-lined channels by the roadside. Since my grandfather's time, some of that water had been allotted to our pond. When the sluice gate was drawn, the water fell foaming into the pond in a cascade, while the fishes tried to show their skill in swimming against the current. I would stand watching, entranced, clutching the rail of the southern balcony. At last one day the pond was filled up with cartloads of rubble. The disappearance of the pond marked the end of that mirroring of a country scene set round with green shadows. The nut tree is still there,

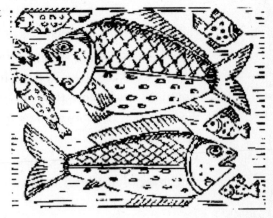

but no one has talked about the brahman's ghost[†] for a long time. There is more light everywhere these days, inside and out.

(*Childhood*, chapter 1)

In our childhood there were virtually no provisions for luxury. On the whole, life was led much more simply than it is now. The modern age would cut off all relations with those times if it saw how little it took gentlefolk to keep up appearances in those days. It was the practice of the times; on top of it, our household was particularly free of the bother of paying too much attention to the children. The fact is, adults amuse themselves by pampering children; for children, it's simply a nuisance.

We were ruled by servants. In order to lighten their work, they forbade us nearly every kind of movement and activity. However stifling that may have been, neglect was itself an enormous freedom: it left our minds free. Our souls escaped the grip of constant feeding and dressing and decking-up.

There was nothing even remotely elegant about our meals. Our clothes[†] were so meagre that it would be mortifying even to talk about them to the young folk of today. I never wore socks on any occasion before I was ten; in winter, one plain garment over another was considered enough. Nor did we ever see this as a misfortune. We only felt sad that our family tailor Niamat saw no need to put pockets in our clothes: there has never been a boy in even the poorest household without some movable and immovable possessions to stuff into his pockets. By God's grace, there is little difference in children's wealth between the rich and the poor. We had a pair of slippers each, but not where our feet would be. With every step we took, we kicked them ahead of us: the slippers moved so much more than the feet that the purpose behind the invention of footwear was frustrated all the way.[†] Everything about our elders was remote from us—their movements, their clothes, their talk, their pleasures. We caught occasional hints of these things, but they were far

beyond our reach. Nowadays youngsters treat their elders lightly: nothing holds them back, and they are given everything even before they ask. We never got anything so easily. Many paltry things were hard to get; we comforted ourselves with the thought that they would be ours once we grew up, and vouchsafed them to that remote future. Hence whatever small things were given to us, we enjoyed to the utmost: from the rind to the core, nothing went untasted. In well-to-do families these days, children so readily get all kinds of things that they take half a bite and throw away the rest. Most things in their world go to waste.

We spent our days in the servants' rooms on the first floor, in the south-east corner of the outer quarters.

One of the servants was named Shyam, a dark and well-built lad with long hair. He came from Khulna District. He would make me sit in a particular spot inside the room, draw a circle around me with a piece of chalk, and warn me with raised finger about the grave danger of stepping outside the circle. He never explained whether the danger was creatural or godly, but he frightened me all right. I had read in the Ramayana about the disaster that befell Sita[†] when she stepped out of her magic circle, so I could not laugh away Shyam's chalk circle either. Just below the window there was a pond with paved steps leading down to it. Near the wall to the east of it stood a giant Chinese banyan tree; to the south was a line of coconut palms. Imprisoned within the chalk circle, I would part the window slats and look at the scene like a picture book nearly all day. Right from the morning, I would see the neighbours come one by one to bathe in the pond. I knew when each would come, and also everyone's bathing habits. One would stop his ears with his fingers, take several quick dips and leave; another would not immerse himself at all, but spread out his towel, fill it with water and pour it over his head again and again; one would sweep the water with his hands to remove any floating dirt, then suddenly dive in; while one plunged in without

warning from the top step of the ghat, making a loud splash. Some
muttered holy verses, all in one breath, as they entered the water. Some
were in a tearing hurry to finish bathing and go back. Others were in
no hurry at all—they bathed in a leisurely way, dried themselves,
changed, shook out the ends of their dhotis two or three times, picked
a few flowers from the garden and then set off home at a relaxed pace,
spreading the contentment of their freshly-bathed bodies in the air. So
the day wore on till one o'clock in the afternoon. The ghat became
desolate and silent. Only the ducks and geese went on diving for
water-snails and busily preening the feathers on their backs.

The great banyan tree would possess my mind once everybody had
left the pond. It had a dark tangle of aerial roots around the main
trunk. There was an enchantment in that shadowy corner of the
world. There alone, nature seemed to have forgotten her usual laws:
an impossible Age of Dreams seemed to reign there in broad daylight
even in the present age, somehow dodging God's eye. Today I can no
longer tell you clearly what sort of beings I saw there in my mind's
eye, or what they did. It was of this tree that I would write one day:

> Standing there with matted locks through night and day,
> Ancient banyan, do you remember that little boy?

Where is that banyan today? Even that pond, the mirror in which the
goddess of the tree viewed herself, no longer exists; many of the people
who bathed in the pond have followed the path of the tree's vanished
shadow. And that little boy has himself grown up, put down all kinds
of hanging roots around him, and sits amid that vast maze counting
the hours of joy and sorrow, sunlight and shadow.

We were forbidden to go outdoors; even inside the house we couldn't
move freely everywhere. So we peeped out at the great world of nature
from crannies and corners. There was something called 'the outside': a
substance stretching endlessly beyond my reach, yet its sights and
sounds and smells crept in from everywhere through chinks in the
doors and windows. It would touch me for an instant, trying by sign-
language to play with me through the bars of my prison. It was free

while I was captive—there was no way we could meet, so the tie of love between us was profound. The chalk circle has disappeared today, but the barrier remains. What was then far-off remains far-off, what was outside is still so. I recall the poem I wrote when I grew up:

The cage-bird had a golden cage,
The forest bird lived free.
They met one day—who can foretell
The plans of destiny?
The forest bird said, 'Cage-bird,
To the forest let's away.'
The captive bird said, 'Forest bird,
In the cage we'll quietly stay.'
The forest bird said, 'No,
'I shall never dwell in chains.'
'Alas!' sighed the captive bird,
'How can I freely range?'

The parapet around the roof above our inner quarters rose above my head. Once I had grown up a little and the servants' rule had relaxed somewhat, when a new bride had entered the household and was indulging me as her leisure-time companion, I sometimes went up there at midday. Everybody had finished lunch; there was a break in the routine of household chores. The women's quarters were sunk in rest; the saris, wet after the midday bath, had been hung out to dry; a flock of crows were crowding round the left-over rice thrown in one corner of the courtyard. In that lonely moment of leisure, the forest bird touched beaks with the caged bird through the openings in the parapet. I stood gazing outwards. There was the line of coconut palms at the end of the inner garden; glimpsed through them, a pond in the neighbouring quarter known as 'Singhis' Garden', and beside the pond the cowshed belonging to our dairy-woman Tara; and still farther away, jostling the treetops, ranged roofs of all shapes and sizes, high and low, gleaming in the midday sun till they faded into the pale blue of the eastern horizon. Here and there on those distant roofs a few stair-top rooms reared their heads, as though raising their immobile forefingers to tell me, with winks and signs, the secrets within them. Like a beggar outside a palace gate, dreaming of priceless jewels beyond all possibility locked up in the treasury within, I imagined those faraway houses as being packed with endless games and untold freedom. The sky blazed overhead, the kite's shrill scream came to my ears from its farthest end. In the lane running along Singhis' Garden, past the silent houses asleep by day, a pedlar went crying 'Bangles, toys, who wants my toys?'—and my mind filled with a great wistfulness.

My father often went travelling; he was rarely at home. His room on the second floor remained shut. I would part the door slats, reach inside and draw back the bolt. Inside, there was a sofa at the southern end. I would spend the whole afternoon sitting quietly on that sofa. To begin with, the room was kept shut for months on end, and was out of bounds; so it had a strong smell of mystery. Moreover, the sun beating down on the empty roof heightened the dreamy state of my mind. There was another attraction too. Mains water had just been introduced in Calcutta. It was a great novelty, still plentiful everywhere in the city, north as well as south; it was supplied unstintingly even to the Bengali quarter.[†] In that Golden Age of water mains, the water

reached up even to my father's room on the second floor. I would turn on the shower and bathe to my heart's content—not for comfort, only to indulge my fancy. The joy of freedom blended with the fear of restraint—between the two, the Company's water rained on my heart like arrows of delight.

However little direct contact I might have had with the outdoors, I enjoyed its charms—the more, perhaps, for that very reason. Too many materials make the mind lazy; it comes to rely wholly on outward things, forgetting that a feast of delight is more an inward than an outward matter. That is the first lesson of childhood. A child's possessions are few

and small, but he needs no more to give him delight. The wretched
child who is given too many toys finds his play quite spoilt.

There was a little garden in our inner compound: it could hardly be
called a garden. Its chief items were a shaddock, a jujube, a hog-plum
tree and a row of coconut palms. There was a round platform of
brickwork in the middle, among whose crevices grass and various
lichens had trespassed and put up their flags like defiant squatters.
Only such flowering plants as could survive without care carried on
with their humble duty as best they could, laying no blame on the
gardener. There was a threshing shed in the north corner; the
womenfolk sometimes went there on housework. This shed has covered
its face and vanished silently long ago, admitting the defeat of the
village way of life in Calcutta. I do not believe that Adam's garden of
Eden could have been in better array than this garden of ours. The
first man's paradise was uncluttered—it had not wrapped itself round
with artifice. Ever since humankind ate the fruit of the tree of
knowledge,[†] his need for decoration and ornament has grown
constantly, and will keep on growing till we have fully digested that
fruit. The garden inside our house was my Eden, and it was enough for
me. I remember that early on autumn mornings, I ran out into that
garden as soon as I was awake. The smell of dewy grass and leaves
rushed to greet me, and the dawn with its soft fresh sunshine thrust its
face through the fans of coconut-leaves swishing above the eastern wall.

There is a piece of land near the northern end of our house which we
still call the barnyard. This shows there must once have been a barn
there to store the year's supply of grain. In those days, town and
village were rather alike, like brother and sister in their childhood; now
that they're grown up, you can hardly see any resemblance.

On holidays I used to run off to this barnyard—not so much to play,
more out of a fondness for the place itself, though I cannot exactly say
why: perhaps because, as a lonely waste space in the very corner of my
home, it had an air of mystery. We neither lived there nor put it to
any use; it served no need. It was outside the house, a bare and useless
piece of land where no one had bothered even to plant a few flowers;

so a child could give free rein to his fancy in that empty space. Any day when I could give my guardians the slip and run away to this place seemed like a holiday to me.

There was yet another fascinating place in our house, but to this day I have not been able to discover its whereabouts. A girl my own age, whom I used to play with, called it the king's palace. Every now and then she told me, 'I went to the palace today!' but I never had the good luck to accompany her. It was a wonderful place: the games they played, and the playthings they played with, were equally wonderful. I had the feeling that it was very close by, either upstairs or downstairs, but somehow I never could go there. I often asked the girl, 'Is the palace outside our house?' She would reply, 'No, it's right here.' I sat puzzling over the problem: I had seen every room in the house, so where could that palace be? I never asked who the king was, and I have yet to discover where his kingdom lay. All I ever learnt was that the king's palace was right inside our own house.

When I look back at my childhood, what I remember most vividly is that the world and life itself seemed to be filled with mystery. The unthinkable lurked everywhere: one never knew when one might encounter it. This idea was constantly in my mind. Nature seemed to hold out her closed fist and say with a smile, 'Tell me what's inside!'— and nothing seemed impossible for sure.

I remember how I planted a custard-apple seed in a corner of the south verandah and watered it every day. The very possibility that a tree

might grow from the seed stirred my awe and curiosity. Custard-apple seeds sprout still, but they do not make the same wonder germinate in my mind any more. The fault does not lie with the seeds but in my mind. We stole rocks from the hillock in Guna Dada's† garden to make an artificial mountain in a corner of our study, stuck little flowering plants on it, and fussed so much over them that they put up with it only because they were plants, and lost no time in dying off. I can't tell what wonder and delight this little hill afforded us. We believed it would be equally wonderful to our elders; but the day we put our belief to the test, our indoor hill vanished somewhere with all its trees. We were full of grief at being taught so brusquely that the corner of a schoolroom was not the proper place to set up a mountain. Our hearts were crushed under the weight of all those stones when we realized that our game diverged so widely from our elders' wishes.

I still remember what an intimate charm the world held for me in those early days. Earth, water, plants and sky—they all spoke to me, they never let me remain indifferent. It hurt me to think that I could only see the surface of the earth and never underneath, so I made one plan after another to take off the earth's brown wrapper. It occurred to me that if a large number of bamboo poles could be driven into the ground one after another, I just might be able to reach the earth's core. At the festival of Maghotsav,† rows of wooden pillars were planted round our courtyard to hang chandeliers from. They starting digging holes for them from the beginning of the month. The preparations for a festival are always an exciting event for children, but these excavations had a special attraction for me. Year after year I saw holes being dug in the ground, deeper and deeper until the whole man vanished inside, and still there was nothing like a passage through which a fairytale prince or minister's son could successfully journey into the underworld; yet every time I felt as though the lid of a treasure chest had been thrown open. If only they were to dig a little further, I would think—but they never did: there was a little tug at the curtain, but it was never drawn aside. I wondered why the elders, who could do whatever they pleased, chose to stop at such shallow depths—if children like us could have had their way, the earth's deepest secret would not have lain underground in neglect for so long. I would imagine likewise that all the secrets of the sky were hidden beyond the blue that one could see. When our tutor said, while teaching us the *Bodhoday*,† that the blue dome of the sky was not an obstacle at all, it seemed utterly unbelievable to me. He said, 'You can build staircase upon staircase and go on climbing for ever and ever—you won't hit your head against anything at all!' I felt he was being miserly in planning his staircase. So I went on yelling to myself, 'More stairs, more stairs!' When at last I understood that would do no good, I sat stunned, convinced that this was such an amazing secret that only teachers knew about it.

(*Memories of My Life*, 'At Home and Out of It')

My father began travelling widely a few years before I was born. I hardly knew him in my childhood. He came home suddenly now and then, bringing with him servants from faraway places. I was always curious and eager to make friends with them. A young Punjabi servant called Lenu came with him once. The kind of reception that we gave him would have done Ranjit Singh[†] proud. He was from a strange land—moreover, from Punjab, which made him very special in our eyes. We held Punjabis in almost as much esteem as the mythical figures of Bhim and Arjun.[†] They were warriors: no doubt they had lost a few battles, but even for that we held their enemies to blame. Our hearts swelled with pride to have a person of such a race under our roof. In my sister-in-law's room there was a toy ship in a glass case: when you wound it up, the waves would rise and fall on a sea of coloured cloth, while the ship tossed on the waves to the music of an organ. I sometimes managed to borrow this marvellous object from Bouthakurani[†] after much pleading and whining, and amazed the Punjabi with it. Because I was caged within the house, everything foreign and faraway fascinated me. That's why I paid Lenu so much attention. For the same reason I felt excited when Gabriel, a Jewish vendor of perfumes, arrived at our gate in his gabardine sewn with little bells; and the giant kabuliwala,[†] in his loose grubby pyjamas and his bags and bundles, held a fearsome mystery for me. Anyway, when father came home we youngsters only peeped and pried around his servants to satisfy our curiosity. We never managed to get as far as him.

The Russians were always the bugbear of the British government. I clearly remember that once in my childhood, the word went round that Russia was about to invade India. A well-meaning woman described to my mother the terrible dangers this implied, as elaborately as her imagination could fashion them. My father was in the hills at that time. No one could tell through which mountain pass the Russian hordes might pour in from Tibet, swift as a comet; hence my mother grew very worried. The rest of the family obviously did not share her concern, because she finally gave up hope of adult succour and turned to me, a slip of a boy. 'Write to your father about the Russians,' she told me. That is how I first wrote a letter to my father, telling him about my mother's anxiety. I knew nothing about the forms of letter-writing, so I in turn approached Mahananda Munshi† in the family office. The format that emerged was no doubt in perfect order, but the text smelt like the dry lotus-leaves of old papers, among which Saraswati the goddess of learning sat in our estate office. I received a reply to my letter by and by. My father wrote that we need not worry about him; he would chase the Russians away himself. I don't think even this tremendous reassurance really convinced my mother, but it certainly made me more bold about my father. I now began to visit Mahananda's office every day in order to write letters to him. Pestered in this way, Mahananda was obliged to draft them for a few days. But I had no money to pay for the stamps. I hoped that I would not have to worry after I had made the letter over to Mahananda: the letters would duly reach their destination. Needless to say, he was much older than me, and those letters never reached the Himalayan peaks.

(Memories of My Life, 'My Father')

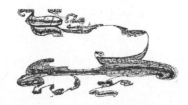

Destruction

Let me give you some fresh news of the world, my dear.

There was this little cottage a few miles from Paris, and Pierre Chopin was its master. It was his life's passion to create new plants—matching strains, crossing pollen grains, fusing taste, colour and appearance. It was slow work: it took years to change the nature of a single flower or fruit. But his patience was matched only by his joy in his work. He seemed to work magic in that garden of his. Red turned to blue, and white to crimson; stones vanished from fruits, as did their rinds. Fruits that took six months to grow began to do so in two. He was a poor man, with no head for business: he would give away costly plants to anyone who uttered a word of praise. Anyone who wanted to cheat him had only to come and say: 'What lovely flowers you have on that tree there! People are coming from everywhere to see them—they're all amazed!'

He always forgot to ask them to pay.

There was another great love in his life, and that was his daughter Camille. She was the joy of his nights and days, and his fellow-worker as well. He had trained her to master the gardener's art. She could graft one plant on another no less skilfully than her father. She would not let him hire a gardener. With her own hands she dug the earth, sowed the seeds, weeded the beds, working quite as hard as her father. Besides all this she cooked for her father, did the sewing, answered his letters—in fact, looked after everything. Their little cottage under the chestnut tree was sweet with peace and hard work. The neighbours

who came to tea in the garden would remark upon it. Father and daughter only smiled and said, 'Our home is beyond price. It isn't made with a king's treasure but with the love of two souls. You won't find another one like it anywhere.'

Jacques, the young man Camille was to marry, sometimes came to lend a hand with the work. He would whisper in her ear, 'When will it be?' But she kept putting it off, for she couldn't bear to marry and part from her father.

Then France went to war with Germany. The laws of the state were harsh and unbending. Even old Pierre was dragged off to the front. Camille hid her tears and told him, 'Don't worry, father, I'll look after our garden with my life.'

She had been trying to create a yellow variety of tuberose at the time. Her father had said it couldn't be done; she had insisted it could. She resolved to astonish him with it when he came back from the war, if she could make good her claim.

Meanwhile Jacques came home from the front on two days' leave to tell her that Pierre had been made a Commandant. He had been unable to come himself, so he had sent Jacques with the good news. Jacques arrived to find that a shell had landed in the flower-garden that very morning. The garden had been destroyed, along with the person who had guarded it with her life. That was the only mercy: Camille too was dead.

Everybody wondered at the advance of civilization. That shell had swept across the sky for all of twenty-five miles! Such was the progress of the times!

The might of civilization has been proved elsewhere too. The proof lies in the dust and nowhere else. It happened in China. That nation had to battle with two powerful civilized states.[†] There used to be a splendid palace in Beijing. It was full of enchanting works of art gathered over the ages. Such wonders had never been worked by human hand before, and never will be again. But China lost the war. It was bound to lose, for civilization is marvellously skilled in the arts of destruction. But alas for all that wonderful art, the loving labours of generations of master spirits! It disappeared who knows where, amidst the short-lived scratching and biting of civilization. I once went travelling to Beijing[†] and saw it with my own eyes. I can hardly bear to talk about it.

—*Translated by Suvro Chatterjee*

Glossary

THE RUNAWAY CITY

Howrah Bridge: The most important bridge joining Calcutta with its twin city Howrah across the river Hooghly. The present bridge began to be built in 1937. When Rabindranath published this poem in 1931, there was only a pontoon bridge or 'bridge of boats'.
Harrison Road: a road in central Calcutta leading to the Howrah Bridge; now called Mahatma Gandhi Road.
Monument: the Ochterloney Monument, now called Shahid Minar.
(Martyrs' Column): a tall tower in the heart of Calcutta.
nagra: a kind of shoe with turned-up points, worn in northern India.

BHOTAN-MOHAN

banana-gourd: the thick skin or shell of a tight-layered bunch of banana flowers.

THE FLYING MACHINE

adjutant bird: a big ungainly stork that (like the common Indian or pariah kite) eats small animals and all kinds of rubbish.

THE TIGER

memsahib: a European woman.

THE PALM TREE

In the original, the tree is specifically the *tal gachh* or toddy palm.

AT SIXES AND SEVENS

quicklime: spread on paan or betel-leaves before adding spices.

chapatis: a kind of flat round bread, very common in India.

THE INVENTION OF SHOES

pandits: men of classical Sanskrit learning.

THE BUILDER

I'm not your Shirish: The little boy speaking in this poem is pretending he is a real builder as he makes his toy houses. But his account of the builder's work is very realistic, and of course the question he asks at the end even more so.

roofbeaters: A roof was traditionally made waterproof by covering it with a layer of special mortar, and having workmen (or often women) beat it with bats until it was hard-packed.

THE BEGGAR'S BOUNTY

Shravasti: an ancient city in the present-day state of Uttar Pradesh. The Buddha lived for long on the outskirts of the city, so that it became a great centre of Buddhist religion and culture.

Anathapindada: A merchant of Shravasti. His real name was Sudatta. He was called 'Anathapindada' or 'provider to the poor'. His unlimited gifts to the Buddha and his religion, and his generosity to the poor, finally left him poor himself. He also joined the Sangha or Buddhist order, so that Supriya could be described as the daughter of a *bhikshu* or 'begging monk'.

THE KING'S PALACE

Nilkamal-Master: Nilkamal Ghoshal, Rabindranath's childhood tutor, who also features in the poet's accounts of his childhood.

MORE-THAN-TRUE

Ush-khush Mountains: Rabindranath moves between real and fantastic names at this point. The cities have real names, or something like them; but *ushkhush* is a Bengali word used of fidgety or restless people.

THE RATS' FEAST

Kalikumar Tarkalankar: Kalikumar was the man's first name. *Tarkalankar* ('ornament to the art of logic') was a title or degree given him for his Sanskrit learning. The name sounds a little like *Kalo kumro tatka lanka,* 'Black pepper and fresh (i.e. hot) chilli'.

The Sacrifice of the Black Pumpkin: Vegetables, especially pumpkins, could be given to gods as offering or 'sacrifice'; but of course the boys are thinking of a more bloody kind of sacrifice.

sugar-balls...sweets: The Bengali refers to *kadma,* crunchy balls of sugar, and *khaichur,* sweetened popped rice rolled into balls.

THAT MAN

Mahabharata: one of the two great ancient Indian epics.

Tepantar: a vast field traditionally mentioned in Bengali fairy tales.

malai: a sweet made from cream.

Barabazar: a market area in central Calcutta.

in these parts: i.e. around Shantiniketan, with reddish soil.

jamewar: a kind of expensive shawl, embroidered all over, made in Kashmir.

Just think, Shrikanta etc.: From a traditional Bengali song called a *panchali* by the famous poet Dasharathi Ray. The song had been taught to Rabindranath in his childhood by Kishorinath Chattopadhyay (see note below).

Chitragupta: the secretary or assistant of Yama, the god of death. It was his task to record everyone's good and bad deeds, to judge them by after their death.

Hindustani ustad: a master-singer of north Indian classical music.

Mohan Bagan: a famous Calcutta football club.

Bhim Nag: a famous Calcutta sweet-maker.

Din-da: Dinendranath Tagore (1882–1935), Rabindranath's great-nephew: a notable musician, one of the chief musical members of the Tagore circle. *Da* is short for *Dada.* Dinendranath was Nandini's elder cousin.

rasgullas: a sweet consisting of balls of curd in sugar syrup.

Barabazar, Bowbazar, Nimtala: parts of Calcutta.

Kumbha Mela: a great religious fair held at Prayag (Allahabad) and Hardwar, and less famously at some other places of pilgrimage—not, of course, at *Kanchrapara*, whch is an industrial town near Calcutta.

Doctor Nilratan Sarkar: (1861–1943), one of the most famous physicians of the time.

jalebis: a kind of lacy fritter dipped in sugar syrup.

chamchams: a kind of sweet.

supari: betel-nut: the nut of a kind of palm, chopped up finely and used as an ingredient with betel leaf or paan.

ghee: a kind of thick butter.

dirty water from his hookah: a chamber of the hookah containing water.

sinful age: the Kali Yuga, the last and worst of the four yugas or ages into which human history was divided in Hindu myth and philosophy.

black face: The hanuman or langur (specifically mentioned in the Bengali) has a black face.

Rai Bahadur: a title given by the British government to Indians who were particularly loyal to them—even (as implied here) by giving them information about those fighting the British to win independence for India.

Smritiratna: a scholarly title: 'the jewel of the smritis' (certain religious texts). *Mashai (Mahashay)* is a term of courtesy or respect. Smritiratna Mashai is a traditional Sanskrit scholar or pandit, thus necessarily a traditional-minded brahman. This makes his fastidiousness about touch and diet quite appropriate, but his playing football or chatting with a doorman just as unlikely.

Ochterloney Monument: See notes to 'The Runaway City'.

Senate Hall: a famous building belonging to Calcutta University, now demolished. It was actually a long way off from the Monument.

The Statesman: an English newspaper published from Calcutta. Its office is close to the Monument, as is the Indian Museum.

Comment vous portez-vous, s'il vous plaît?: (French) 'Please, how are you?'

Sankhya philosophy: one of the six great schools of ancient Indian philosophy.

remedy: There were many traditional penances to remove pollution and loss of caste. Of course these would be found in the Sanskrit scriptures or Hindu almanacs, not in Webster's English Dictionary.

Bhatpara: a town near Calcutta, traditionally the home of many Sanskrit scholars. The pandits there would have been able to advise Smritiratna Mashai.

twig toothbrush: specifically of the neem tree; a traditional practice.

Ganesh: the elephant-headed god of wealth and wisdom. People are often named after him. Ganesh is also held to have written the ancient epic Mahabharata to the poet Vyasa's dictation; so the Man is actually paying the writer a compliment by comparing him to Vyasa.

to Cardiff for a game of cards: The Bengali, necessarily, has a different pun: 'I went to Tasmania to play *tas*' (Bengali for 'cards').

Privy Council: the highest judicial authority of the British Empire, where lawsuits could be referred from India in the days of British rule.

bizarre story: The Bengali refers to *adbhuta rasa*. This is one of the nine *rasas* or poetic veins prescribed in ancient Sanskrit poetic theory. The *adbhuta rasa* is the poetic vein of the marvellous or wonderful. But *adbhut* in Bengali commonly means 'strange' or 'bizarre', and Rabindranath is jokingly using the word in this everyday sense.

Kishori Chatto: Kishorinath Chatto (i.e. Chattopadhyay or Chatterjee) was actually an employee of the Tagores in the poet's own childhood. He was the particular assistant and travelling companion of the poet's father Debendranath. Once a professional folk singer, he taught the young Rabindranath many songs. Rabindranath is fancifully transferring to Pupe his own childhood companion.

Ravana: The demon-king of Lanka in the Ramayana, who stole away Sita and was defeated by Rama. He was said to have ten heads. Presumably Pupe had heard the account of Ravana's death in the Ramayana the previous evening.

a rabbit fancier: The dark spots on the moon are sometimes thought to make up the shape of a rabbit.

Brahma's zoo: Brahma, the first of the three main aspects of the Hindu godhead, is the creator of all things. (Vishnu is the preserver, and Shiva the destroyer.)

Bangama bird: Bangama and his wife Bangami are a mythical bird-couple appearing in Bengali fairy-tales.

Seven Sages: the Indian name for the constellation of the Great Bear or Plough.

fields of sleep: The Bengali refers to Tepantar. (See above.)

Jatayu bird: a legendary bird, featuring in the Ramayana. A friend of Rama, he tried to prevent Ravana from carrying Sita away, but was killed by him. He did, however, convey the news to Rama before dying.

squirrel...Rama's bridge to Lanka: In the Ramayana, Rama builds a bridge across the sea in order to reach Lanka and destroy Ravana. (A line of rocks in the sea at this point is supposed to be the remains of the bridge.) All the animals helped Rama to build the bridge: even the little squirrel brought small pebbles.

Diwali: the festival of lights.

Chhatrapati: a word meaning 'king' or 'ruler', specially applied to the Maratha ruler Shivaji. But it literally means 'lord of the umbrella' (i.e. royal canopy), and thus suits Sukumar's make-believe horse.

Satya Yuga: Literally, 'age of truth': the first, ideal yuga or age of human existence according to Indian legend. (See note on 'Kali Yuga' above.)

THE WELCOME

zamindar: landlord.

your daughter: a Bengali pun here. The Bengali word for 'girl' or 'daughter' is *meye*, which the zamindar confuses with 'MA'.

a marriage: another pun. *Biye* in Bengali means a marriage or wedding.

THE POET AND THE PAUPER

Kunjabihari: 'he who walks in the garden'.

Bashambad: 'devoted, obsequious, flattering'.

dal: pulses, lentils.

THE ORDEALS OF FAME

Ganat parataram nahi: (Sanskrit) 'Nothing is greater than music.'

donation...throwing me out: a Bengali pun here. *Chanda*, a subscription, is linked by sound (though not origin) to *chand*, the moon. And to give someone an *ardhachandra* or 'half-moon' means to throw him out by the neck. Kangalicharan is saying something like 'I wanted the moon but you gave me only a half-moon.'

paan: betel leaf.

tanpura: a stringed instrument used as an accompaniment by Indian classical singers.

tabla set: the pair of small drums used to accompany Indian music.

khayal: one of the four major forms or modes of north Indian vocal music.

tappa: another of these major musical forms or modes.

Shori Miyan: the man who first developed and popularized the tappa. His real name was Ghulam Nabi (late eighteenth/early nineteenth century).

MY CHILDHOOD

paan: betel leaf.

memsahib: a European woman, supposed to be lacking in the traditional modesty of Indian women.

darwan: a doorkeeper, hence a guard.

siddhi: a kind of home-made intoxicating drink.

our tutor: This was Aghornath Chattopadhyay (Chatterjee), a medical student who taught Rabindranath English from 1869. 'Our' refers to Rabindranath, his elder brother Somendranath and his nephew Satyaprasad Gangopadhyay (Ganguly), son of the poet's sister Soudamini. Both these boys were two years older than Rabindranath. The three were brought up and schooled together.

shankhchunni: a kind of female ghost.

Magh and Phalgun: i.e. late winter and early spring.

brahman's ghost: a *brahmadaitya:* the ghost in the nut-tree referred to earlier.

our clothes: Actually, the Tagore household accounts show that the young Tagores' clothes were not as few or austere as suggested here.

all the way: a Bengali pun on *pade pade*—literally, 'at every step'.

Sita: During their forest exile, Sita was once left alone by her husband Rama and his brother Lakshmana. Lakshmana drew a line round her for her safety and forbade her to cross it. But she stepped across it and was snatched away by Ravana.

even to the Bengali quarter: The northern part of Calcutta, where Bengalis and other Indians chiefly lived, had far worse services and amenities than the European quarter to the south; but there was enough water even to supply this 'Black Town'.

ate the fruit of the tree of knowledge: a reference to the fall of Adam and Eve as told in the Bible.

Guna Dada: Gunendranath Tagore (1847–81), younger son of Rabindranath's uncle Girindranath and father of the artists Gaganendranath and Abanindranath.

Maghotsav: a festival set up by the Brahmos held in the month of Magh.

Bodhoday: a primer of knowledge for children written by the great scholar and reformer Ishwarchandra Vidyasagar.

Ranjit Singh: (1780–1839), a great Sikh leader and ruler of Punjab.

Bhim, Arjun: two of the five Pandava brothers, heroes of the Mahabharata.

Bouthakurani: elder brother's wife.

kabuliwala: an Afghan trader or pedlar. Rabindranath has a famous short story about a kabuliwala.

Mahananda Mushi: The Tagores' 'munshi' or clerk. His name was Mahananda Mukhopadhyay (Mukherjee). Prashantakumar Pal, Rabindranath's recent biographer, has found evidence that the mother's anxiety lay elsewhere. She had been alarmed by an unfounded report in the magazine *Somprakash* that her husband had given up his family and worldly concerns to lead a spiritual life in the Himalayas. Unable to express her fears openly, she had thought of this means to get news of her husband. It also appears that Rabindranath's immediately older brother, Somendranath, was involved in the letter-writing.

DESTRUCTION

two powerful civilized states: We cannot be quite certain which two states
Rabindranath has in mind. One, no doubt, is Britain; the other might
be the United States, Russia, or even Japan.

I once went travelling to Beijing: in April–May 1924.

Note on Translators

Sukanta Chaudhuri is Professor of English at Jadavpur University.

Suvro Chatterjee teaches at Xavier's School, Durgapur.

Sankha Ghosh is a noted Bengali poet and critic. He retired as Professor of Bengali from Jadavpur University.

Sukhendu Ray retired as Managing Director of Guest Keen Williams Ltd.

Note on Illustrations

The drawings and sketches by Rabindranath Tagore, Nandalal Bose, and Asit Kumar Haldar are from the following sources: Rabindra Bhavan, Visva-Bharati, and Bengali 'textbooks' such as *Sahaj Path*, *Chharar Chhabi*, *Chitra-Bichitra*, *Galpa-Salpa*, *Khapchara*. The doodles are from Rabindranath's manuscripts.

The paintings are by Rabindranath Tagore, Rabindra Bhavan, Visva-Bharati.